Reaching the Young Autistic Child

Reaching the Young Autistic Child

Reclaiming Non-Autistic Potential through Communicative Strategies and Games

A Practical Resource Book
for Parents, Nursery Workers,
Early Years Teachers and Others

Sibylle Janert

FREE ASSOCIATION BOOKS / LONDON / NEW YORK

TO IMO

First published in 2000 by
FREE ASSOCIATION BOOKS
57 Warren Street
London W1P 5PA

Copyright © Sibylle Janert 2000

The right of Sibylle Janert to be identified as the author of this work has been
asserted by her in accordance with the Copyright, Designs and Patents Act 1988.

A CIP catalogue record for this book is available
from the British Library.

ISBN 1 85343 498 1 pbk

09 08 07 06 05 04 03 02 01
10   9   8   7   6   5   4   3   2

Designed, typeset and produced for Free Association Books Ltd by
Chase Production Services, Chadlington OX7 3LN
Printed in the European Union
by TJ International, Padstow

Contents

Preface

My thanks go first of all to all the children, parents, families and staff I have met, talked to and worked with at the various nurseries, playgroups and schools over the past ten years or more. This book is a tribute to them and others like them. It was their sense of bewilderment, helplessness and often despair, as well as my own, that spurred me to research all I could about the puzzling phenomenon of autism, to be able to take back new insights and bits of understanding each week to the children and adults at the special needs nursery where I worked for over six years.

This book would never have happened without the dynamic, insightful teaching, patience and encouragement from Trudi Klauber, then director of the Donald Winnicott Centre, Hackney, now senior child psychotherapist at the Tavistock Clinic, and my sincerest gratitude goes to Trudi for all her time and dedication. Trudi read several of the early chapters, and the book contains many traces of our discussions and thinking together.

This book is also a tribute to Anne Alvarez, senior child psychotherapist and co-convenor of the Autism Workshop at the Tavistock Clinic, and her wonderful book *Live Company* (1992) which had a huge impact on me, both professionally and personally, with its inspiring insights into the inner worlds of very troubled children. Anne's honesty about the struggles the adult (*any* adult: professional, worker, parent, and so on) faces in this work and the value of admitting to one's despair, helplessness and other difficult feelings as possibly a communication from and about the child, was liberating and empowering to me. On a personal level, it affected my relationship with my father and was the topic of conversation of my last meeting with him in the 'pink cafe' on a rainy autumn afternoon before he died a year later. It was probably the only psychoanalytic book he ever read (and read with interest and, I think, recognition). I am grateful to my father for passing on to me his tenacity, his linguisitic interests and his sense of familiarity with academic matters.

The books by Frances Tustin, and especially Sheila Spensley's book *Frances Tustin* (1995), also influenced my thinking greatly by providing a conceptual platform on which to stand, and from which to try to make sense of seemingly incomprehensible autistic behaviours, in order to establish practical strategies, games and 'ways that worked'.

Many thanks are also due to everyone from the Infant Observation Course at the Tavistock Clinic and elsewhere, especially the seminar leaders, and Margaret Rustin, Maria Rhode, and Gianna Williams in particular. I am deeply grateful to the two families who welcomed me so generously every week for two years to observe the development of their babies from (before) birth, and with that the very beginnings of social, communicative and symbolic development, including the joys, preoccupations and anxieties that accompany these early psychological stages.

The writings by C. Trevarthen, D. Stern and B. Brazelton, and especially the videos by Dr Hisako Watanabe, Tokyo, and Dr Stella Acquerone, from the London School of Infant Mental Health, on their successful short-term work with avoidant infants and their parents, made a deep impression on me, and influenced my work and thinking deeply. I also have the ethologist and autism specialist Dr John Richer to thank for his contribution on instinctive traces and internal conflict in human beings from an evolutionary perspective.

A great thank-you also needs to go to all my friends for their support and tolerance of me and 'The *** Book'. I am grateful to Andrew Bottrill for his careful reading and comments on several of the early chapters and to Ruth Shelley, who read the entire early manuscript, for her never-ending support and encouragement. The later manuscript incorporates comments and suggestions from Jean Duggleby, special needs teacher, and Steven Faughey, support worker, who both found several of my games and strategies useful in their work with an autistic child. My special thanks to Bill Austen, who meticulously read the entire final draft for the few grammar and spelling mistakes he could find, and his enthusiastic response to my writing on a topic he had not thought he would find so 'gripping'. Last but not least, I am most grateful to my mother, Imogen Janert, without whom this book would of course also not have come about, for her continuing interest and willingness to help.

Foreword

by Miriam Stoppard

A newborn infant comes into the world able to recognise the human face and dying to relate to another human being. So does the baby destined to be autistic.

The same newborn infant will, even before the cord is cut, focus on your face with stillness, alertness and intense concentration, especially if you bob your head, nod and speak in a theatrical, sing-song voice. So will the autistic neonate.

In the first few minutes after birth a baby will 'converse' with body jerks and fish-feeding mouth movements if he can see your eyes alight with interest and your smiling mouth shaping words. The same goes for the autistic baby.

Babies are born wired to respond to the human voice and the more musical, rhythmic and high-pitched the better. The human voice, especially a running commentary of chatter, is music to every baby's ear, including that of the autistic baby.

And here Sibylle Janert has discovered the bridges any adult can build to help the autistic child attempt, what for him is his most difficult task – to emerge from his internal world and engage with another person.

Her thesis is irresistible because it is grounded in such basic neonatal physiology. And her logic is irrefutable: if an autistic child is born with the instincts and equipment to relate to others, then intervention must begin early (at least by nine months) to keep the apparatus in working order.

The difficulty for parents of autistic babies is figuring out what they can do to help their children. Being the parents of an autistic child can be hard, leading to frustration and low morale. Professional help is not always adequate. Two-thirds of parents see three or more professionals before they get a firm diagnosis; one quarter see five professionals or more. Half of parents feel that autism is explained badly or not at all, so they end up feeling inadequate and powerless.

Parents, take heart. Sibylle Janert has simple, useful suggestions that you can put into practice as your baby grows. They are easily within your grasp. Every baby responds to eye contact – being the focus of attention. Babies love theatricality – the exaggeration of emphasis and action. They can easily latch on to the distinguishing features of objects if we point out wide differences through opposites, soft/hard, rough/smooth. To all babies music, sing-alongs and clapping games are irresistible, making responsiveness a reflex.

Parents can take comfort from the fact that their autistic baby will be helped by all these same things. But whereas the average baby only enjoys them, the autistic baby actually *needs* them. To the autistic baby they are essential vitamins, without which he will not thrive and most importantly will not discover the joy of relating to the people and the world around him.

Sibylle Janert has provided parents with the means to help their autistic child enter the real world.

Introduction

When I started to work with autistic children I searched in vain for a book that focussed on the early years, was practical, child-centred and easy to read, helped the reader to understand what might be going on inside an autistic child's mind and what some of those puzzling behaviours might mean. This book is trying to be what I couldn't find

Parents want most deeply to be able to help their child, if only they knew how, and the sense of helplessness which befalls them when faced with their child's unresponsiveness needs addressing in a practical way. This book tries to give some encouragement through its attempt to shed a little light on some of these difficult feelings. It also hopes to help all those involved with autistic children to recover a little at a time from the trauma and despair engendered by the shattering impact of the diagnosis of autism or 'autistic features'.

Autism is a complex condition of pervasive developmental delay. Parents have usually been aware for some time that something is 'not quite right' with their child long before his first birthday. Not that there is anything one could see: he looks perfectly healthy, is growing and gaining weight. He *can* do lots of things. The trouble is, he just *will not* do them. He simply is not motivated to cooperate. While his physical development is age-appropriate, his intellectual/cognitive development and all social, communicative and emotional development are severely delayed.

What is missing is something we feel just can't be missing in another person, however young, that is, for human beings, whether adult, child or baby, to be interested in and wanting to be with other people. It is the *wanting* that is so unbelievably absent in the autistic child: wanting to communicate, wanting to know, wanting to cooperate. He does not seem to want any of this! He does not look into people's faces to share what they are looking at, and he does not point at things he sees to share his experience, as would be typical for a baby from about nine months onwards. He may be withdrawn and content to be alone for unusually long periods of time, or active and constantly on the go. He may be clingy, climbing onto anybody's lap, or insisting on being picked up by no matter whom.

He does not play like other children of the same age, creatively putting things together for pretend-play, imitating or making up situations in imaginative ways. This seems to be replaced by an often intense interest in objects, which is repetitive, obsessive or stereotypical. His 'play' is more a fiddling with objects – mouthing, banging, shaking, spinning, lining them up, flicking switches. He wants to have, hold, chew, eat things. If thwarted, he may fly into a screaming rage or tantrum, only to return to his activity with an almost tyrannical determination.

Most significant is his overall lack of interest in meaning and symbolisation, for example pretend-play in the home-corner, with the farm or pretend-feeding teddy, which other one-year-olds engage in. Instead his attention is focussed on sensual rhythmic experiences and skin sensations like touching, stroking, handling, and mouthing toys, objects or parts of himself. Perception too may be used to satisfy a sensual way of seeing or hearing, stripped of meaning. While he had seemed to be deaf when spoken to, he may have been concentrating on the humming of the fridge. All awareness of his surroundings appears to have drained away, and he may appear totally lost, as if he had given himself over entirely to the sensation he feels on his skin, for example his hands, his mouth, his back on the floor. He may appear totally lost to the world around him.

Because of his inability to see meaning and to make sense of what happens in the world around him, the autistic child clings to routines and insists that things must always be the same. He may develop odd or stereotypical habits, such as flapping his hands, rocking or rhythmically jigging an object, strongly resisting attempts to get him out of such self-absorbed states. If anything disturbs this order of things, he may get terribly upset with long screaming attacks or inconsolable tantrums, sometimes apparently without a reason that is obvious to the observer.

He has no desire to share how he feels or thinks about an experience, and words and language do not usually interest him much for creative communicative use, if at all. He may be mute and never learn to speak. If speech does develop, its onset may be delayed until the age of five years, and lacking a certain human aliveness and responsiveness: it is likely to be repetitive or 'echolalic', so that he may simply echo your question instead of giving an appropriate answer. He may use words only when he wants something, almost as if saying a word is like pushing a button that will switch on the mechanics of the TV or produce a chocolate biscuit (that is, a person).

The approach of this book does not describe a comprehensive method, but a collection of useful ideas, activities, strategies and games, that evolved through daily hands-on experience using 'anything that worked' including many of the excellent cognitive/behavioural methods currently available, findings from baby research, and modern psychodynamic thinking. It regards an interaction model as essential, because the real problem is seen to lie in what goes on between an autistic child and another person – or not. The aim is to help the child to get involved in human communication through 'adult behaviours' that virtually 'make' him pull all his senses together to focus his attention on interaction with another person and to have such fun doing so, that he is motivated to seek out more of such human interaction. *The first three to four years are the most crucial in terms of intervention for a child with autistic behaviours, and this needs to happen with real strength that comes from and is supported by understanding as early as possible.* The suggested task of the adult is to make an enormous effort to develop and support what there is, or might be, of any healthy developmental potential, by 'reclaiming' it (Alvarez 1992), while at the same time trying to discourage anti-developmental behaviours and autistic anti-mental attitudes, that may already have become habitual and addictive to the child. The book combines thinking with practical suggestions, and encourages a feelingful approach as opposed to automatic mechanical approaches, with the aim to enhance, enliven and humanise behaviour modification techniques by making sense of underlying intra-psychic patterns.

Especially if help comes early enough, ideally as early as nine to eighteen months, and certainly well before the child's fifth birthday, at least some of the earliest foundations of communicative language development can usually be laid to counteract severe developmental delay or even arrest, and carers can be given some firm understanding and, most of all, hope. Whether he will get much or only a little better, learn to speak or not, to play, to read and write – no one can say. The best we can do is try our best, and wait and see.

Written for all those directly involved in the care of a young child described as 'on the autistic continuum', as having 'autistic features' or an 'autistic spectrum disorder', this book has the busy carer in mind, who has no more time than what fits into a tea-break. Some of it will also be relevant and useful with the ADHD child (Attention Deficit Hyperactivity Disorder), and with older children and adults. Sections are kept short, with practical examples and descriptions. While they try to address specific issues, they are not intended to give definite answers, but to support readers to feel confident to use their own understanding and to tailor their responses to each individual child.

Part I outlines innovative practical suggestions for more general management and adult behaviours that help the child's development. Part II describes formats of simple interactive games and activities, tried and tested in years of practical 'on-my-hands-and-knees' experience. Part III tries to make sense of what may be going on inside the autistic child's mind when engaged in his 'autistic' (non-)activities.

All the children described are between three and five years old, unless otherwise stated. Their identity has been changed to guarantee anonymity.

Although very different, they have all been diagnosed at renowned and respected UK diagnostic centres as: 'autistic', 'on the autistic continuum/spectrum', 'with autistic features', 'with ASD' (Autistic Spectrum Disorder).

Because autism is so much more frequent in boys than in girls 'he' is generally used to refer to the autistic child, while the adult is usually referred to as 'she', as there are (regrettably) still more women looking after young children than men.

PART I

ADULT BEHAVIOURS
THAT HELP THE CHILD'S DEVELOPMENT

1
Face-to-face Play and Shared Attention: Where Language Development Begins

'Lets have a laugh together':
The Communicative Delights of Playfulness

Everyone responds well to a light-hearted non-confrontational approach, and so does the autistic child. Wanting to teach him something requires his cooperation with *our* ideas – not often forthcoming. We can tell him to hang up his coat, sit down, do an activity. But the success rate of such an approach is low: he takes no notice, runs away instead of sitting down, struggles or goes limp instead of hanging up his coat or doing the activity. He cannot bear the intrusion, panics and withdraws into his familiar shell of insular cut-off-ness. But if we can join him and be where *he* is at, if we can tune in without making too many waves, just blending in, then we can perhaps, very slowly and gradually, effect some change. Our chances increase if we make any of the above into a playful game. Even if we don't succeed, at least we will have had a game and a good time together, with some social communicative contact.

People sometimes think that autistic children's difficulty with play means that they cannot have a sense of humour, and no interest in it either. In fact, most are as able to respond to playful contact as any young baby. But while the normally developing baby does so much of the initiating and teasing himself, with the autistic child all the initiating (and to begin with much of the responding too) needs to come from the adult, who has to make a much greater effort to emphasise, or substitute, the social and good-natured element in the interaction. Instead of being able to expect him to respond, the adult has to role-model, as with the tiny baby, the child's possible responses *as if* she were pretending to be the child. The adult may need to 'become' the playful and imaginative child she has in mind, to give him an idea of his own potential. She may even have to take on both roles, modelling her own as well as the child's imaginative or playful responses.

Babies do not play symbolically, yet they clearly like teasing and antici-patory games like 'I'm gonna getcha' games (see chapter 4). Like most baby games, they are about sharing a joke by playing around with arousing curiosity, expectations or desires in another person, with no other aim than to have fun. They are about establishing a rhythm between adult and child, with a pinch of surprise added – and then stretching, breaking and remaking it, playing around and 'mucking about' with it, being 'cheeky', 'being a tease'. They involve nothing more than an understanding of the playful quality of the players' communicative intentions, as in the earliest 'looming games' (see chapter 6) we intuitively play with tiny babies:

> Her attention firmly focussed on the baby, the adult suddenly pulls back her head, then swoops forward, saying perhaps a dramatic 'Oh, what a lovely baby!', maybe touching noses, or retreating again before doing so, or ...

Purely social games like these looming games develop into 'I'm gonna getcha games', played with babies from three months: the adult repeatedly pretends to tickle his tummy, bite his nose and so on, much to the child's mounting delight. The fun is in establishing a predictable pattern, which then becomes the stuff to be played and mucked about with, with a little thrill of surprise, an edge of anticipation: it's *slightly* dangerous, but not too much.

In 'I'm gonna getcha' games the adult raises the child's expectations, and then either disappoints or fulfils them in unpredictable ways: 'perhaps I'll catch or tickle you now, or not quite yet, or now, or here, or maybe ...', creating a good-natured atmosphere of anticipation and suspense, with the child on small tenterhooks, or as if 'walking the tightrope between fear and delight' (see chapter 4).

Normally, children surprise their parents at an early age by being 'cheeky' themselves. From around seven to eight months onwards, they begin to tease other people quite 'deliberately' for no other effect than to engage in playful social relationships and interaction games:

> Pat (twelve months) discovered that standing in front of the TV brought 'hilarious' results from those family members watching TV, Emily (eight months) developed a shrill shriek to get her parents' attention, and Paul (ten months) would crawl towards the plug, stop when mother said 'No!',

quickly move towards it again, stop when told 'no', looking back with a mischievous smile, over and over, and much to his mother's alternating amusement and irritation.

Unfortunately, this is not a description of baby life with an autistic child. It is possible that the absence of such cheekiness, teasing and attention-seeking behaviour could provide us with our first serious hunches that something is not quite right with a child's social and communicative development as early as seven months (Reddy in: Whiten 1992).

But the autistic child's lack of initiating does not mean that he is also unable to *respond* to such playful teasing games. There may be traces of such playful cheekiness that are so weak, so faint, so unexpected, that we have never noticed them. Can we alert him to such social communicative delights? Adults sometimes miss an autistic child's tiny attempts at playfulness, communicative teasing or earliest pretend-behaviours, because they do not expect such 'baby communication' from a four-year-old:

Tyrone was placed with no additional support in a friendly main-stream nursery class with thirty children, one teacher and two classroom assistants. He wandered aimlessly, and then developed aims of his own. Perhaps not surprisingly, these were largely hostile and destructive, liberally peppered with adults shouting 'NO!' from a distance. He poured glue into the pencil boxes, sand over the books, 'painted' floor or wall next to the easel, swiped at children. He would go to the door, each time looking around for an adult's shouting reaction, a grin on his face. He discovered that standing on something allowed him to open the high door handle and run out, as if wanting to get out of what to him must have seemed a hostile environment.

His teachers were desperate. Together we realised that Tyrone could not manage on his own (and nor could they), and arranged for one adult always to be with him. They also made sure that they stopped shouting at him. They felt he had been teasing them with his deliberately provocative behaviour. He was challenging them to help: things were not well, and could they, please!, urgently do something about it. He said it with a sense of humour. But they had only seen the defiant aspect of it, got cross and shouted.

With surprise and relief they saw how positively Tyrone responded to a playful approach, the use of surprise as in 'I'm gonna getcha' games (see chapter 4) and unexpected friendly reactions. Instead of shouting, they found that if they whispered his name in an ominous-sounding mock-threatening way, for example pretending to be absolutely 'horrified', he would look up with disbelief and relief, smile and stop his irritating attention-seeking behaviour. He had been looking for attention outside the classroom. Now he had the attention he needed inside: he could stop seeking it.

The moment his teachers made the monumental leap of shifting their focus from looking at Tyrone's behaviour as an irritating nuisance to understanding it as a communication from him to them, things looked very different. Now there was an interactive social game between adults and child. Tyrone's behaviour also suggested that his hope for understanding was still alive: he had an idea of something good, or better, and he was determined to get to it. Perhaps he would find it on the other side of the door?

Playful interaction, cheekiness and warm, friendly teasing rely on nothing more than a sense of uncertainty and curiosity, created by challenging the other's assumptions, by surprising them with a reaction, which may be unexpectedly sudden, unexpectedly slow, unexpectedly dramatic, unexpectedly whispered, or different, obviously 'wrong', silly, 'over the top', or pretending to be something which it is not. It is about togetherness and communication (so different from the cruel bullying kind of mocking or ridicule, done to put the other down, not 'with' but 'against' them), and defined by friendly cooperative sharing between two people: one can only be cheeky if there is someone to be cheeky to; one cannot tease without having someone to tease.

Because it engages an instinctive response, pretend-threat as in 'I'm gonna getcha' routines commands all the autistic child's awareness and attention. It virtually 'makes' him pull all his senses together in order to locate this perceived threat and to prepare for an appropriate escape. The quick succession of approach and retreat, of 'will she – won't she?', of larger-than-life pretend-threat and exaggerated withdrawal, creates a humorous and ambiguous situation which he can only 'defuse' by looking at the other person's face for clues of their intentions, feelings and expectations. This means that in order to check what the other is likely to do next, even the autistic child is drawn to look at the adult's face. In order to remove the tension of excited-anxious uncertainty, and to regain a state of emotional equilibrium, both baby and autistic child use any clues from the other person. The playful nature of the interaction means that they are motivated and interested to find out what the adult has in mind, whether her intentions are friendly or scary, whether she is smiling or grim-faced. Such searching for and spontaneous use of emotional meaning in another's facial expression as a guide in ambiguous situations is what is so crucially missing in the autistic child. Because his interest and curiosity are provoked by the adult's surprising and unpredictable actions, and held for as long as the ambiguous 'perhaps, perhaps not' situation continues, the child is engaged in 'shared attention'. Together with the child's looking for clues in the adult's face in what is called 'social referencing', these are the essential prerequisites for language development.

It does not matter who starts off the game. Often it takes the adult to look for or catch the moment, the glance, the smile, the sound, the grin, the tiny movement – then *not* to feel over-enthusiastic, but to suggest, playfully, to perhaps try something, ... or not, ... or ...

The adult's movements may be slow – but suddenly she may pounce and tickle him – or stop dead, again surprising the child who was all prepared for her to come and 'get' him. The child might run away – then suddenly stop, to look back laughing – or let himself be caught. The adult may ask him to put on his coat, but then put it on the 'wrong' child or pretend to be putting it on herself, thus egging him on into some otherwise unusual purposeful activity of getting his coat back and onto himself, or, the child may run away laughing, in his version of the 'come and get me if you want to put my coat on' game. The adult may offer him a spoonful of food, holding it in mid-air without moving for a long time, and then, just when he thought she was going to force-feed him, put it back on the plate or eat it herself ...

It is probable that the child had indeed felt somehow threatened but not enough to run away. There was something odd about this so-called 'threat', it didn't quite fit: it was coming at him and disappearing, too fast for what would instinctively qualify as a serious threat. The moment he was ready to retreat or run away, the threat itself retreated. What was going on here? Where had it gone? The child cannot retreat safely, because that threat is still hanging around somewhere. So he's got to look. The repeated sudden disappearance of the 'threat' coming at him draws his attention to it, his curiosity is engaged, his mind alerted, his senses drawn together into one focus – so unusual for the autistic child – and so good for him.

All these playful or cheeky teasing games lift the interaction out of such functional purposes as wanting to have or get something, for example, food, a toy, a coat on or one's own way, into a purely social communicative playing-field, a pure playing with intentions and feelings. They live off creating and removing doubt, in rapid alteration, in the other person. They feed off smiles in each other's faces, movements and gestures, they create uncertainty and curiosity out of thin air, they play with each other's expectations and intentions as with juggling balls. Provided the adult creates a situation that is ambiguous enough to arouse curiosity, carefully scaffolded in an atmosphere of friendly affection, then most autistic children cannot help but join in and interact socially in ways that might have been believed impossible. The window of opportunity with some young autistic children is that some hibernating capacities have been lying dormant, waiting to be awoken and reclaimed through simple moments of playful contact, that can thrill and enliven the passive or withdrawn child, and the despairing or worn-out adult too.

Your Face – The Best Cause-and-Effect Toy Ever Invented: Always the Same and a Little Different

Better than any toy, the human face can be as exquisitely responsive and expressive as nothing else in the world. It is really the most amazing cause-and-effect toy ever invented: it has eyes that blink, that can shine and widen in surprise, in joy, with love, concern or worried urgency, they can narrow in a more pained or nasty expression, be that real or pretend. It has a mouth that can not only talk and sing, but also make funny, surprising, soothing, exciting shapes to watch and noises to hear; it can open and shut, purse and smile, blow raspberries or make plopping noises, with a tongue inside that can wiggle from side to side, go in and out. It has a nose that can crinkle or blow, that sticks out so one can grab it, to which Mummy always says one of her frequent 'no's (!).There are eyebrows which can frown or stretch in surprise, or mock anger, teasingly provoking a laugh and fostering a dawning sense of humour.

Already, newborn babies prefer to look at anything with three dots within a circle, like the most schematic version of a face, for example the socket in the wall, a car from the front with its two big light-eyes and teethed grill-grin, even the three legs of an upside-down colander, or the washing machine with its round knob-eyes and huge round mouth greedily devouring great amounts of washing. Most autistic children respond to such 'face schemas' too, and some research suggests that face recognition could be innate to all humans and higher mammals (Carpenter 1974, Stern 1985, Trevarthen 1977, 1979, and others).

> Newborns, only ten minutes old, can copy opening their mouth or sticking their tongue out in imitation of someone facing them at the 'ideal distance' of twelve inches. A newborn can be seen to concentrate on her father's face with an obvious effort to copy what he does with her tongue or mouth, while his tightly focussed attention provides the baby with a mental scaffold to help her focus. It is the attentive human con-nectedness, expressed largely in the adult's face and eyes, that enables this tiny baby to pull together all her senses and powers of observation

in an as yet unprecedented effort and into one unifying experience of herself. After several attempts, the baby unmistakably 'mirrors' the adult's mouth movements, her face showing at the same time signs of great satisfaction, at having 'done it'. These must be amongst the earliest traces of a sense of self in the way of 'I did it!', of feeling 'This is me!' and 'I can do it!'.

But how can a ten-minute-old 'earthling', with no previous experience of human beings and faces, which she sees for the first time in her life, 'know' that she has a mouth, that her mouth or tongue are the same as Dad's who is making these faces at her? How does she know how to coordinate her facial muscles to perform such complicated imitations, having had no time for learning? She must have brought at least vestiges of such knowledge and abilities with her already when she arrived on earth ten minutes ago.

If being human means being born with the instinctive ability to recognise faces, this includes autistic children. And although it is possible that some autistic children are born with a defect in this innate human potential, or that they acquire such a defect later on, there always seem to be at least vestiges of this human endowment on which to build. To test this I made about thirty simple schematic drawings of different faces which, stuck on card, could also be used for picture-posting, copying and lotto games:

All the autistic children who were shown these faces showed considerably more interest in them than in other pictures. Several children who were not usually interested in pictures showed a surprisingly definite preference: Adrian would reliably pick out one of the few faces with especially bright beaming eyes, Fatima preferred laughing, Billy cross and angry faces. The first lotto game he played with interest and concentration was the faces lotto.

Pre-verbal children with a mental age of under one year respond to the high-pitched, exaggerated and larger-than-life manner mothers all over the world use to speak to their babies, called 'motherese' or 'parentese'. This includes most young autistic children, who, despite their reputation for avoiding eye contact, can be engaged by a human face, provided we are highly sensitive to exactly what we are doing, for example subtle changes in distance, speed, size of facial movements, of tone, timbre and volume of our voice, of the noises we make and variations, and of the child's most subtle responses. The adult needs to be totally focussed and highly mentally alert to the child's feeling-states as expressed in his face and body language, providing the same supportive 'scaffolding' a newborn needs. When speaking with a very young infant, the sensitive adult speaks in a high-pitched voice and clear simple rhythms, using alerting consonant sounds like 's', 'sh', 'p', 'ff', 'ks', 'x', 'ps'. She may speed up when she feels his attention waning, or make her eyes bigger or brighter in response, to intensify his attention and keep it focussed on her face and on their inter-action, for as long as possible. She is highly attuned to the baby's responses, and adapts what she does, and how she does it, carefully to his feeling-state. Brazelton, the famous paediatrician, describes how a mother manages to engage and hold the attention of her premature and non-responsive tiny baby, highlighting the effort that is required from the adult. Because of his particular difficulties with pulling his senses into one single focus of con-centrated attention, the autistic child needs our focussed help so much more and for much longer.

> The mother takes on facial expressions of great admiration, moving back and forth in front of him with great enthusiasm; or, again in response to an unmoving infant, she takes on an expression of great surprise, moving backwards in mock astonishment; or, in the most exaggerated manner, she greets the infant, and, furthermore, carries on an animated extended greeting interchange, bobbing and nodding enthusiastically exactly as though her greeting were currently being reciprocated. (Brazelton et al. 1974)

What attracts and holds the attention of both the baby and the autistic child more than anything else, is that faces are always 'the same but a little bit different'. His mother's face is a baby's first experience of what is called 'self-deformation', that is, something that although it moves and changes does not lose its overall shape or form, like for example a squeaky rubber duck. Although there is something constant and unmistakable about a person's face, it is also always a little different, for instance when one is happy, or sad, cross or tired, with glasses or make-up, or without, or a different hairstyle. A talking face moves differently from a laughing, shouting or whispering face. Something is almost always happening in a lively human face, usually in a pattern, or rhythm, of gradual build-up to some kind of climax, before ebbing off. All the parts of a human face move in myriads of subtly different ways that can be totally responsive to the child, whether in timing or content – or deliberately contradicting expec-tations. Babies are well-known for noticing, and being interested in such tiny differences – which can also be observed in the autistic child's sometimes obsessional attention to detail.

A similar attraction to that of 'self-deformation' is the fascination with mobiles, the glittering leaves or branches of a tree moving in the wind, his own flapping hands or the patterns of the movement of people moving about around him:

Tyrone and Adrian loved looking out of the window for long periods. Tyrone's mother thought he was watching the tree outside. Derek and Simon were both fascinated by the rhythmic flapping or jigging movement of some string-like object, that stayed the same but also looked a little different all the time.

Where the movement of a human face differs from those of the tree, mobile or toy is that these are without meaning or aim, without purpose, intention, expectation or social awareness. They simply go on and on. In the tiny baby's earliest experience of the world, before he has developed a notion of expectations and meaning, the most important thing is a sense of ongoingness (Ogden 1992). What gets the tiny baby to develop a grip on his own mind, in a meaningful, purposeful and interested way, is his mother calling him 'into relationship' again and again, through face-to-face interactions and social games.

All later language development and social understanding depends on a baby's earliest communicative experience with his main caregivers. The autistic child has, for whatever reason, not built those very early foundations of social communication. But without being interested in communication, there can be no talking, no meaningful listening, no interest in looking at another person's face. Before a child, autistic or not, can progress to the more sophisticated levels of spoken communication, he therefore needs to catch up with these earliest foundations of human contact and communication, i.e. the early face-to-face games with a devoted parent who tries to respond to what baby *is already doing*: if the baby's actions (including his burps, twitches, vocalisations, and so forth) are treated *as if* they were purposeful, they do indeed become purposeful and intentional, crucial for meaningful communication and speech development. Getting a response to his sounds or facial expressions is to any young child a life-affirming experience, every time again confirming his sense of 'I am, because I have an impact, because I can *make* another person respond to me.'

While a toy is not responsive to anyone's feelings, the human face can do all that toys can do and so much more. It can also suddenly and surprisingly stop, to create a planned effect or to provoke an intended reaction. As soon as this has succeeded, or backfired, the human face is back again with a completely different bag of tricks. One can never quite know what is coming next, anything is possible – because behind the scenes of a human face is a person with something in mind, who will notice and respond meaningfully, and in the best way she can, to what she thinks is happening. An adult may even feign crossness, or the urgency of extreme and imminent danger, when she notices the child slipping into his cut-off state of mind. Sometimes the urgency of her voice reaches him and helps him to pull himself back from the brink, to 'reclaim' him into human company.

Only a person can 'reclaim' a child whose mind has drifted off into the far-away states of cut-off-ness. Static objects, such as toys, lend themselves far less to this. They also hold the danger of the child becoming 'hooked' and, yet again, slipping away from playful social communication.

Eager to try to make contact with a withdrawn or cut-off autistic child, adults sometimes use a toy to attract his attention. But their efforts are usually short-lived: he is not interested, turns his head away, averts or closes his eyes, witholds any detectable response as if he didn't see, hear or notice. Waving the object may attract his attention a little. But then even that fails, and the adult gives up in helpless frustration – perhaps to try again later, probably with the same meagre results, or the autistic child may become obsessed with the toy itself – and again social contact is lost.

But when 'talking' to a three-month-old, few adults would wave a toy. Most intuitively attract the baby's attention to their own face to engage him in face-to-face play. The toy only obscures the best and most versatile, the most human, responsive and stimulating multi-purpose toy, which is always with us, which can never be broken or lost or forgotten: our face. Many adults do not make enough use of their face to engage the attention of a three- to four-year-old autistic child, saying 'I never thought of it':

If the child is keenly looking at our face for more action, we can provide him with more dramatic facial expressions, sounds and noises. If he has turned his head away in avoidance, we can slow down and move our head back, until he looks back to see where the hell it has gone, at which point we can catch his eye and interest again, more gently now and more quietly, before moving in again, just a fraction less than before, with big smiles and some surprised and friendly noises. It is in our face too that we can express our concern when he continually turns away from our attempts at making contact. We can even express acceptance and an understanding of such withdrawal, combined with continued interest, and even determination to find exactly the right level of contact and stimulation: he may just catch a glimpse of this in the split seconds in which his eyes tear past ours, or in which his mind is connected enough.

'Make it Bigger!':
How to Catch, Reclaim and Hold his Attention

Autistic children do not usually concentrate and pay attention. But most *can* do it! There are certain times when every young autistic child I have met does manage to pull his senses together into one coherent focus: for some it is food, for others a toy or activity (often obsessional or repetitive). This suggests that he does not altogether lack the capacity of pulling his senses and attention into one single focus. This is an important observation. But most of the time he does not do it – or he cannot do it by himself, or does not want to or know how to. Our aim is to help him expand this capacity as much as possible.

What attracts someone's attention? What do you do to attract someone's attention? How do you know you've 'got' it? What do you want it for, in the first place? Once you've got it, what do you do with it? How do you hold someone's flagging attention? How do you get it back, once it has drifted off? These are observational experiments we should study carefully, as they can teach us a great deal about ourselves, about what attention is, what we want to achieve, how, and what for.

After many years of working with autistic children, Anne Alvarez, a child psychotherapist, suggested the term 'reclamation' for what we are trying to do, i.e. to claim, or reclaim, him as a fellow human being with all the human potential that belongs to being human. To help us with this there are a number of adult behaviours that seem to be 'innately pre-programmed' in human beings to achieve this better than anything else. The most important is to 'make it bigger', that is to make a conscious effort to be dramatic, to exaggerate what we do or say, down to the smallest details. By over-acting our responses we make our communications to the child 'bigger', and easier for him to attend to.

Big expansive movements, a voice pitched to match your gestures, greatly exaggerated in space and time, help him to see easily that you are attending to him. He may try to avoid seeing it, pretend with all his might that nothing is happening. He may dig his mental heels in thinking 'No! I'm not looking. I cannot see anything. I'm not coming!'

But if you make 'it' big enough, as big as you can, so big that you feel like the silliest over-the-top amateur actor there ever has been, while also showing the most intriguing obvious delight – then he won't have a chance: you can arrange things in such a way, set the scene for an inter-action that is soo intriguing, sooo exciting, soooo fantastic, that he just has to have a look!

If we speak and act in a theatrical and larger-than-life manner, by using expansive gestures and exaggerated pitches in our voice, tuned precisely to each child's preferences and abilities, it is virtually always possible to claim the attention even of a very withdrawn child. Even a whisper can be made bigger, either by exaggerating the whispering or the quietness of your voice, by slowing it down more, or accompanying it with some slow and deliberately attention-getting faces or gestures.

Some of this is similar to how we instinctively help a tiny baby to focus. How do we attract and hold a baby's attention, or regain it, if he has turned his head away or disintegrated into crying? The answers are in watching the details of babies' communication, watching someone who is 'really good with babies', paying attention to what holds the baby's attention, makes him coo or laugh or turn away, and what the adult does to hold or regain it. Much of this relates to what the adult does with her face and head, with her voice, breath and body movements, with lots of 'making it bigger'.

A sensitive adult wanting to strike up a 'conversation' with a baby of about three months might first attract his attention with a sharp in-breath, which may be voiced with an 'as-if-alarmed' and super-surprised "h-aa!?' It may almost sound as if she just had a tiny version of the fright of her life (with some children, it may need to sound like a big version of the fright of her life). The alarm in someone's voice seems to provoke an innate compulsion to check her face: is there really an immediate threat to her life in it? The child looks up, but finds the alerting sounds embedded in a broadly smiling greeting-face, with wide beaming eyes, welcoming him with delight into a communication game, claiming him as partner and into a human encounter.

At this moment the pre-verbal child's attention has been caught, his curiosity stirred. Such curiosity acts as a 'central cohesive force' (Frith 1989), needed to 'concentrate' his attention. There is suspense and anticipation: what will happen next? How can we hold and extend this attention for as long as possible, and engage him into the interactive 'dance' that is the essence of communication? Because of the autistic child's habit of letting his mind and senses disintegrate into a state of non-seeing, non-hearing or non-attention, our efforts have to be so much bigger: more pronounced, long term and consciously dosed. Something new and interesting has to happen all the time, with movement within a continuous building-up, peaking and letting-off of suspense and tension. We need to exaggerate in as many different aspects as possible: in time and space, in voice, face, movement, gestures, in terms of variation in speed and tempo, mouth shapes, eyebrows and eyes showing varying degrees of mock surprise and frowns. Everything can be exaggerated and 'made bigger': how loud, exciting or fast we speak, how slow or surprisingly we move, how much our face changes or expresses excitement, alarm, unpredictable suspense, and so on.

Such facial displays are characterised by the fact that they form slowly, as if in slow motion, and are then held for a long time. They gradually but dramatically build up to the fullest display, often ending in a surprising sound or tickle, kiss or touching of noses. The adult usually begins with an exaggerated greeting posture with a facial expression of mock surprise with eyes and mouth open very wide, eyebrows up, head raised and slightly tilted up as if asking a non-verbal question with a sharp in-breath of 'ha'!? The variations on this are endless, with all kinds of smiles or pursed lips, with one eyebrow up, the other down, or both up at first, then slowly bunching up into a fierce pretend-frown. The head may move towards the child, or a little to the side, chin up, or down, or forward and immediately back to indicate the intention of approach, followed by instant withdrawal to demonstrate that we are not being pushy.

The movement indicates both the aliveness and unpredictability of human interaction, which is what commands the child's attention to remain focussed. He finds himself in a situation where he feels 'you never know – I had better keep an eye on it' – which means on *you*. This is of course exactly what we wanted to achieve in the first place: the child is now not only focussing his attention, but he is focussing it on another person and is involved in human communication. We want to make this interchange as much fun as possible, to whet his appetite for more of such interaction and communicative attentiveness.

Widening of eyes and mouth, voiced in-breaths and other expressions of alarm and unexpected surprise, have an innate signal value. It is alarm, of any shape or form, that instinctively commands attention and alertness without fail. Wide eyes are universally understood to indicate a general readiness to interact together with a heightened focus of alert attention on the other. Movements of the mouth serve to maintain the interaction, especially if it involves a widening of the mouth. Vocal sounds can also be expressive of this. These innate response patterns are used by mothers all over the world. Young children and babies need adults to help them regulate early interactions, to learn to figure out what is important to focus on, which allows the child to enter into the realm of human and social communication.

The three-year-old autistic child has had almost three full years of, often insistent, practice in *not* focussing, *not* pulling his senses together, *not* paying attention, *not* studying mother's face – a very long time when brain growth is at a biological peak. Adults can easily succumb to his bizarre behaviours, losing all confidence in being able to claim his attention, to engage his interest in social activity. It is important to be aware of this, as such feelings need to find their match in our massive efforts to claim, or reclaim, his attention and interest. We have years of anti-developmental practice to counter. That is how much bigger we have to try to make all our overtures, all our gestures, all our communications. Make whatever you say, do, or show him 'about three or four years bigger'. We need to make our presence unavoidable for him, but in such fun ways, as not to put him off, should he risk coming out of his shell.

The 'make it bigger' principle also applies when the face is not the main agent of communication:

With the child who never stays in one place for long enough, or who is so avoidant as to never look directly at someone's face, dramatic movements made in the field of his peripheral vision may catch his attention. We may walk past him, or move our hand past his line of vision in such an exaggeratedly slow or suspenseful way, stopping all of a sudden and utterly unpredictably, that his attention is simply commanded by the suddenness of the surprise. He simply *has* to shift his eyes and attention because our unexpected attention-grabbing movement startled him into alertness.

We can also make everyday activities and gestures 'bigger': we can show him his coat on its peg as if it was the most exciting thing we ever encountered: 'Wow! Looook! Your – (pause of the "I can't believe this! This is just sooooo exciting!!" nature) – your coooaaat! There's your coat!' How much more exciting to be now allowed to put it on!

The same approach can be used with any piece of clothing, dressing and undressing, with shoes, socks, hat and gloves. Dramatise the activities in the bathroom, with washing, toothbrush, toothpaste, potty and toilet. Every single gesture at the table can be 'made bigger' and include unexpected little surprises, to jerk even the most far-away child out of his mental slumber:

To get Kofi to look up, the way we pass the bowl of food or the juice needs to be much 'bigger' than with Patrick or Tyrone. The bowl or jug may need to approach him in a huge swoop, coming from one side and across his field of vision, only to move away again immediately, in order to gain his protesting attention for it. But now we've got it! He is protesting because he has now seen it, and he wants it. He does not want it to pass him by. At this moment his attention is on it 100 per cent.

A word of warning may be due here: 'making it bigger' does not simply mean more, louder and faster. We want to exaggerate whatever will draw the child's attention to the *feeling* that is shared and expressed by the behaviour, rather than simply the behaviour itself:

> One adult would approach Kofi by talking to him in a barrage of loud, shrill noise. The more he withdrew, the louder and more persistent she got, the closer she would sit, holding his hand harder, whenever he wanted to run away.

While she may have used the idea of 'make it bigger' she did so without *sensitivity to the child*. Her approaches lacked the element of playfulness, so essential to win his interest and willingness to cooperate. She forgot to observe her own behaviour, or Kofi's likes and dislikes (he hated any loud, and especially shrill, noises), and to tune in with him on his level of development. Sometimes 'making it bigger' may have a paradoxical feel, like moving exaggeratedly more slowly, or more quietly, or more unexpectedly:

> It helped Cheng to be given very explicit clues especially with one's voice and face, which usually meant talking more softly and much more slowly to him, rather than louder and faster as the eager adult was often prone to do without noticing. To engage his attention it helped if the adult behaved *as if* she was talking about something unbelievably interesting, speaking in a very exaggerated, but at the same time slow, drawn-out and low voice, that stretched his attention and held his interest.

Approaching the autistic child with 'make it bigger' in mind at all times provides the adult with a simple 'technique' of not falling prey to the sense of being rendered non-existent, so common and demoralising. If tuned precisely and sensitively to each child, this technique, intuitively familiar to all of us from talking to much younger babies, can achieve an enormous increase in the success rate of the autistic child's responsiveness, his ability to pull his attention together and his motivation to focus.

What's in a Mouth?: On Rekindling Instinctive Interests

Many young autistic children 'have a thing about' eating and food, about mouths, teeth, chewing and biting – either seeking or avoiding awareness of their mouth. Some bite everything they can, so toys have to be restricted to those that can safely be bitten and chewed; others seem to avoid using their mouth at all, whether for eating, biting or chewing food, or for exploring the different parts of their mouth for vocalising and babbling. Later, some bite themselves, often their hands, a sign of frustration not often seen under the age of four years, while biting other people can become a problem much earlier.

The mouth is one of the main points for making contact with the outside world for all living beings, human or animal. The newborn baby uses his mouth first to cry, then to search for something he has never known, found or experienced before. When his mouth finds the nipple, he knows instinctively 'this is it', how to suck and what to do. For a long time the mouth remains the baby's primary place for making contact with and exploring the world, and he will try to suck and mouth everything. His mother's mouth already fascinates the newborn, with its continuous changes and her voice which he recognises from before he was born. It is with our mouth that, as tiny babies, we first learn that we can bridge a distance: we can call a mummy, who is gone, to come; we can tell the world that we are upset, hungry, frightened, lonely, angry, or happy and content. From about four months, a baby also begins to babble and respond to Mother's cooing sounds by cooing back, feeling nurtured by such purely mental–emotional stimulation. Increasingly babies' hands and fingers become more important for exploration. But our mouth never quite loses its prime place: it is the great gateway into ourselves, bridging the gap between self and other, between our own body and the world outside. We use it to talk with each other, for singing, crying, kissing, for eating, biting, chewing, whether to still our hunger or for comfort, for smoking, drinking or taking medicines.

But with the autistic child the mouth often seems like the gate to a one-way street, leading nowhere but into his narrow, autistic inner world, with no possiblity for two-way traffic. The outside world of toys, objects, people and food gets bitten up, chewed and swallowed. Sometimes the one-way system seems to work the other way round, and sounds, bitten-off bits of toys or unwanted food are spat out. Things that 'stick out' are got rid of. Yet, the mouth is also the link to the non-autistic world, a much under-used opportunity to rekindle his instinctive interests. Few people think of letting a five-year-old autistic child really explore their mouth, and stay with it, as they would with a seven-month-old. But if their attention is drawn to the adult's mouth, many young autistic children display a rare curiosity, a desire to explore and to be in direct contact with another person. This also facilitates face-to-face and intimate communication:

One day, Tim was lying around absentmindedly sucking the top of his T-shirt as usual. I sat by him trying to engage him into an 'I'm gonna touch your nose!' game with a 'wiggly worm' finger, when suddenly he went as if to bite my finger. He had never done this before, and I was more delighted than shocked by so much initiative and direct communication from such a passive child. In response, I went *as if* to bite his finger (but didn't), pretend-growling at him playfully and showing my teeth, smiling and talking normally inbetween to help him differentiate pretend from real (that is, the kind of baby games people naturally play with tiny babies, but do not write about). I had never felt him to be so 'there', so aware of another person, so interested, alert, active and interactive. He was using his eyes as if really taking in and processing what he saw – and for such a long time, perhaps five minutes.

Tim was both trying to avoid my 'biting' and to stick his finger into my mouth. The pull of these two opposite interests seemed to enable him to focus and hold his attention, giving him some kind of thrill and excitement. He was particularly interested in my open mouth and my pretend-biting, sticking his finger into my mouth *as if asking* me to bite it: holding it there and looking me straight in the eye. I could not but feel it as in invitation: after all, this was Tim who usually avoided all (eye-) contact. When I did pretend-bite his finger slightly, just so that he could feel a little of the hardness of my teeth, as opposed to the softness of the rest of a mouth (as one does with an infant), he laughed. Instead of running away or cutting off, it spurred him on to try and bite me again. He asked for more. So I made a big pretend-shocked fuss, taking on what I thought could be his role, what *he* could be feeling and justifiably do in response, that is in an 'as if'- kind of way. He did it again and again. When he drifted off, I could get his attention by pretend-biting him with laughing-growling noises – and he would go as if to bite me in turn: he would have bitten me, had I let him. But as it is the adult's responsibility to make sure that no one gets hurt, it remained a game.

This development of an interest in an interactive game and something like a sense of humour in Tim was wonderful. He wanted to explore my mouth with his finger, especially my teeth (their hardness?). Repeatedly he indicated, either by opening his own mouth while egging me on with his eyes or with his fingers, that he wanted me to open my mouth, so he could see into it: a major revolution with a child who usually required such enormous effort and perseverance to engage at all. Suddenly here was something, my mouth, that interested him greatly, that he was motivated to explore with his fingers, eyes *and mind*, which of course also meant that he was looking into my face and there was much communicative eye contact.

The mouth is, of course, most important around food and eating, an area where even the more passive autistic child often shows an unusually high degree of motivation – another opportunity for developing his interactive skills. With a clear idea of the communicative aspect of playful cooperative teasing in mind, fed largely by notions of 'pretend' and 'as if', even the autistic child can hardly fail to respond. Every time this happens he will experience himself able to communicate and, if he enjoys it, to want more. Mohamed's interest in mouths and teeth surfaced during a cooking session:

> Mohamed had been mixing flour, sugar and margarine for some time with a wooden spoon. The other children had been eating and licking the cake mixture, but Mohamed had made no attempt himself. I wanted to ask him about this, but he has no language. So I tried to ask him by playfully taking the wooden spoon to his mouth *as if* to feed him (but with no intention of actually doing so), making exaggerated eating noises while saying 'Hm! Nice!' He instantly turned his head away in absolute horror. I then pretended in a dramatic way to eat it myself, which made him look back tentatively and as if in total disbelief. He returned my smile with surprise.
>
> At that moment our new game was created: I would pretend I was going to 'feed' him with that big wooden spoon (without ever touching his mouth!), his face would light up like the sun, as it does, knowing that I would not actually perform my pretend-threat. There was good eye contact, and he kept 'asking' for more by looking at my face. He watched me eat bits, with a mixture of horror, interest and curiosity, 'asked' me to open my mouth by touching it and peering into it with great intent and curiosity, also feeling my teeth tentatively. Around the table, there were other adults and children talking. Then, suddenly, my words broke off and everyone burst out laughing: the wooden spoon was in *my* mouth. Mohamed had switched roles. He had done to me what I had pretended to do to him. He grinned. I was amazed: Mohamed had understood the game, taken his turn, paid me back – and he knew it!

While initially terrified that I might force-feed him, Mohamed realised with relief and delight, that I was in fact offering a game. At first he had been scared of an intrusive spoon. But by watching my face he began to trust me not to put the spoon into his mouth. He was fully motivated and emotionally engaged in a social communicative game. He began to understand the meaning of 'pretend', the first step towards symbolisation, and enjoyed our game so much that he kept asking for more. It was Mohamed who wanted us to take turns. We were both enjoying something together, a game, a joke, humour, laughing, with some first beginnings of the possibility of identifying with another person. Here was an autistic child, who was aware of the presence of another person, another mouth, another mind, which he wanted to explore.

Mealtimes have the potential to be great communication times: eating, socialising and talking go very well indeed together. But the autistic child does not seem to know this. Adults who are relaxed about food can make great use of this sitting-down time for communicative games, as long as these enhance the child's focus on the *eating game's* main purpose, that is food and eating, not running around or smearing sticky hands over tables, clothes, settees, or winding up adults.

Patrick rarely ate anything at nursery, although he explored the food on his plate with his fingers. When offered food on a spoon, he turned his head away. When he realised it was only a suggestion, that no one was going to *make* him eat anything, he relaxed. Soon, he turned the 'game' around, wanting to feed the adult with the food she had offered, which meant looking into the adult's face to get the spoon into her mouth. I know a number of autistic children who absolutely love doing this. After some months of this Patrick ate several foods, for example mashed potato, having checked their safety first by feeding them to another person. Many autistic children can be helped to understand such playfulness in the eating situation especially:

Hold out some food near the child's mouth *as if* about to feed it to him, while also showing clearly, with a broad smile and a relaxed, playful, laid-back manner, that you are not in the least bothered whether he eats it or not. Demonstrate by withdrawing or wiggling the spoon, by moving it back and forth a little in a quick rhythm, that you have no intention whatsoever of pushing anything into his mouth without his consent. In this way, even the autistic child is compelled to look up into your face to see what you are up to. Because that perceived threat, spoon, food or whatever, keeps coming and going, he is unsure what is happening. 'Is it or is it not getting at me?' So he looks up to check, voluntarily seeking communicative eye contact with another person for social clues.

The communicative attention of most autistic children can be engaged by games that focus on their own mouth or that of others. This may even include the mouths of toy crocodiles, dolls and teddy-bears. Mohamed often used a glove puppet as if it was biting him or other toys, and when a toy dog was brought in, he examined its tiny open mouth with unusual interest. Patrick became very interested in 'mouth and face games' and later learnt to speak.

2
Talking, Singing, and Communicating for Two

'If Only He'd Talk, He'd Be Alright': Being Able to Copy Words is Not Talking

The autistic child's 'speechlessness' seems to be the most obvious difference from his age-mates, and people often hope: 'if only he'd talk, he'd be alright'. Teaching someone to say some words does not seem to take much. But despite daily efforts, the autistic child usually does not begin to talk. If he *does* learn to say a few word-like sounds, he does not use these 'words' spontaneously to communicate like other children his age. Is something wrong with his mouth, throat, teeth or tongue? Is it a sign of his autism? Is the teaching method at fault? Should the adult persist with her training?

> Wanting to teach Tyrone to speak, his mother held a bag of crisps high above her head saying 'What is it? What is it?! Crisps, Tyrone! Say Crisps, Tyrone! Crisps!! What is it? CRISPS! Tyrone, say Crisps! Crisps!! ...' Tyrone, his eyes firmly fixed on the bag, jumped to reach them, straining, whingeing and yapping, but made no speech-like sounds.

We don't know exactly how language develops in the autistic child, if and when it does (Ricks 1975, Tager-Flusberg 1981). But all *communicative* language development must follow the same pattern. Before speech can develop, the child must have become a good communicator without words. Without being able to communicate, words have no meaning. Without meaning they have no communicative value. After all, some people use sign language just as effectively to communicate and 'talk', because they, or their parents, are deaf. Parents often complain that the autistic child needs daily sessions with a trained speech/language therapist. But even a trained speech therapist cannot *teach* him to talk. Even if he can say some words, this does not mean that he will use them, or even that he understands what they mean. He needs first to catch up with the basics of communication, necessary for all subsequent speech development. These develop only in interaction with another human being, and out of the baby's early communicativeness that needs no words:

At nine months, Anushka picks up a teddy while crawling around. She makes babbling noises, then looks up and smiles at me. Holding teddy, she pulls herself up to stand by her pram, looks round at Mum, then to me, smiles, stretches up with great effort, as if wanting to put him into the pram, too high for her to reach. She makes straining noises and turns to her mum, who now comes over and says: 'Oh, you want to put teddy in?' Anushka looks back and forth between Mum, pram and teddy, straining more, which feels like a confirmation of her mother's question. Her mother puts teddy into the pram. Anushka lifts up her own arms, looks at Mum making straining noises again. Her mother understands, lifts her up and says 'Look, teddy's in Anushka's pram.' Together they look at teddy. Anushka points her finger and says 'Da!' Her mother agrees 'Yes, teddy. Teddy is in your pram.'

At ten months, Anushka crawls to the stairs, very fast, then stops, looking back at her mum with a wide expectant grin. Her mother swoops her into her arms, laughing, and kisses her. 'This is her new game: she *knows* she is not to crawl up the stairs by herself, and she keeps teasing me about it. Sometimes it gets really irritating. But really it's so sweet', she explains.

When a child begins to speak, words take their place alongside other communicative gestures he is already fully fluent with. It cannot be the other way round, just as one cannot paint a house before it is built. The very beginnings of language lie in the moments when a mother follows with her eyes what her baby is looking at and joins him in this. Unlike the autistic child, Anushka is an efficient communicator who 'speaks' confidently via gestures, straining noises and communicative looking. Her mother has no difficulty in understanding what she means, putting Anushka's communications into words. In fact they have a complex conversation. Anushka has clear ideas about what she wants to do with teddy. She calls her mother, asks for help and engages her in real teamwork: to put teddy into her pram, and to be picked up herself to see him together. Her 'word' bore little resemblance to the actual word 'teddy', but her mother understood, 'translated' and agreed.

For a long time, the adult needs to home in on whatever the child, or baby, is interested in. A child can only learn to speak and use language, once he has a firm understanding of the importance, and the joys, of such a mutual focus on a common topic, of 'shared attention'. In a way, mother and baby are having a 'looking conversation': the baby's silent eye-pointing may be a question that says 'Can you see what I am looking at?' His mum may answer with 'Yes, it's a butterfly. A lovely butterfly! Oops – gone! Where is it gone?' In this way the baby gradually comes to understand that what he is looking at has meaning for his mum too, and she calls it 'butterfly'. He comes to love sharing attention like that, and he wants to know what she thinks of things. He checks her face to see whether something is safe or dangerous, allowed or not, bringing a smile or a frown as response. This is called 'social referencing', the next stage on from 'shared attention'. This is what autistic children find so very difficult, or fail to establish, and where the roots are for their not having learnt to talk. This is where we have to apply our nurturing, our most focussed attention, because without these foundations all other efforts will have little meaning and effect.

Most crucial for a child to learn language is that the adult firmly believes in the child's communicative intent, i.e. being so focussed on the child, that one interprets and responds to all his actions and vocalisations (and non-vocalisations) *as if* they were a clear message: to see everything the child does, even the tiniest movements, as deliberate messages from him (even if they aren't!), all his utterances at least an attempt at communication, and to follow the child's eyes to see what he *could* mean.

Anushka's teasing game relies largely on 'social referencing': she checks her mother's face for her reaction, and then either obeys or deliberately disobeys her mother's message. Without words Anushka shows her mother that she knows that her mother knows that Anushka knows, that her mother does not want her to climb those stairs, and she does it just for the heck of it, just because it gets them to have so much fun together. Many autistic children do also understand and use this kind of communication, and can be reached on this level.

But any ordinary development can be interrupted, blocked or led astray by a variety of factors, and it is helpful to keep in mind that in the young autistic child two processes occur simultaneously: the normal course of human communicative and language development, and the autistic tendencies that try (often successfully) to pull this off-course. While these need to be kept in check with appropriate teaching approaches by the adult, we must also make the huge effort to encourage or push his maturational capacities for communicative language development without their being wiped out by autistic anti-tendencies.

The autistic child needs to learn to have a good time being, or mucking about with, another person. If it's fun he'll want more. If he wants more, he'll ask for it – and asking for something is communication. At that moment he will be communicating because he wants to, not because you are telling him. A child who does not communicate does not need to learn to say words – he needs to learn to *want* to communicate. If he does not want to communicate, he will not speak, even if he did have the words and language to say it. And if he did want to communicate, but could not speak (like the deaf child), he would point to things, using eye contact and gestures, to try to make you understand what he has in mind (like Anushka). Our aim must be to show him that communicating with another person is fun.

Having fun and enjoying doing something together is what was missing between Tyrone and his mum. Although they seemed to have a common topic of conversation (crisps), it was really more of a misunderstanding: Mum wanted him to use his mouth to say the word 'crisps', he wanted to eat whatever she was holding out of his reach. Whether he ate them or not, she did not care, while he cared about nothing else. From his point of view, she seemed, for some incomprehensible reason, to be tantalising him with 'Look, I've got crisps. But I am not giving them to you!' It is true that Tyrone did not try to figure out (as another child would) what his mother wanted. But neither did she pitch what she was doing to what he might have been feeling, wanting, needing, or even what he may have been trying to say or do. They were at cross-purposes, their communication gone astray: Tyrone did not understand what his mother wanted and she did not understand why he did not obey. So she missed Tyrone's communication.

Had his mother been focussed on what Tyrone was trying to communicate (i.e. his 'communicative intent' = wanting to eat the crisps), she might have been more responsive, perhaps talking to him as to a much younger baby: 'Oh, you want these *crisps*, Tyrone. "Please, mummy", says Tyrone, "give me those crisps." Come, let's sit down on the settee together and open them. Do you want to have a go? Open!, Pull! ... Oh, dear, Tyrone can't open them. Shall we do it together? Lets open those crisps!' "Hurry up, mummy", says Tyrone, "I want my crisps." There! Opened it: there are Tyrone's crisps! Yum yum, crisps. Crisps all for Tyrone.'

In this way, she would have been helping him to do something *he* wanted to do, while giving words to what he might have been thinking, wanting and feeling. As adults we need to make an effort to fit our words and responses to what the child is trying to communicate. This kind of baby communication makes the word 'crisps' stand out (being mentioned seven times). Gradually, she may leave out the last letters of the word 'crisps', waiting expectantly and creating a suspenseful tension to encourage him to finish the word himself. Things have to be felt as making emotional sense, to fit like hand into glove, like a crying baby into mummy's soothing arms, like an anxious question finding a sensitive and receptive ear. It made no sense to Tyrone to be asked to say 'crisps', when his mother was saying it herself all the time already, and because all it needed for him to get them was to pull down her arm, or snatch them from her hand.

Had the crisps been up high on a cupboard next to some biscuits or fruit, then just jumping would not have been good enough. In this case, his mother could well have insisted he 'say it', waiting patiently for any sound or gesture, as with Anushka's 'da'. Or: standing in front of the closed cupboard where they both know crisps and other favorite foods are kept, there would be a real need for him to communicate when she asks 'What do you want?' After all, it may be chocolate he wants today, or a biscuit. She may help him by starting the sentence for him to complete, stretching the bow of excitement and suspense for as long as it will go, for example: 'Tyrone wants some [expectant pause] cr— (?) Yes, cr-isps – Tyrone wants crisps.'

In our attempts to teach the young autistic child to speak, we have to make this enormous effort to create communicative situations of 'shared attention', that feel nice and make emotional sense to him, because they are on the level of his mental development (often of a baby between two to eight months):

We would not tease a nine-month-old with his bottle by holding it within sight but out of his reach, expecting him to understand that we want him to say 'bottle' or make a similar sound before giving it to him. Instead we would give him the bottle and talk to him, or carry him to the kitchen to look for the bottle together. At other times we copy his sounds, and play babbling and cooing games with him. Then he may copy our sounds, to recreate the memory of our nice time together. When he has progressed sufficiently from this early level of communicative development, enjoys our company and social games, and communicates well non-verbally, he will one day surprise us by saying 'bottle'.

Because of the autistic child's developmental delay, we need to focus on the early baby games that practise pure communication and dialogue skills: we do not need words to have a conversation. If we copy his sounds, he is likely to respond with delight and echo them. At that moment we are having a dialogue, a babbling-conversation. We would have no problem doing this with a four-month-old. So we can do it with the autistic four-year-old, and have fun. The more often we can draw the autistic child into situations of shared attention in ways he enjoys so much that he wants more of it, the better.

Don't Go Silent Too – Talk to Him :
If Only Because it Keeps You Alive and Thinking

It is not uncommon for the adults to become as mute, and even non-communicative, as the autistic child in their charge. When asked why, the response is often a helpless 'but he doesn't understand', 'I don't know what to say' or 'I don't understand what is going on.' Although understandable this is not necessarily logical, as not understanding does not need to make us unable to speak. By not responding in the usual human ways which we take for granted, the child behaves as if the adult was not there. Feeling baffled is a normal human response, and the adults' experience of utter puzzlement has perhaps resulted in something like a mental blackout that affects their usual common sense and thinking capacities, i.e. 'I just can't get my head around it.' It is like a state of shock – shock over the child's puzzling and humanly incomprehensible behaviour, one's own inability to make sense of it, to communicate or even to make contact, and the experience of apparently having lost one's own mental capacities, even though one thought they were usually working well enough.

> I vividly remember the sense of bewilderment in Leila's support worker sitting silently, and as if paralysed, by the computer while Leila was involved with some marbles on the floor. When I spoke to the support worker, she came 'back to life'. Her intention had been to let Leila play on the computer. When I suggested that it might not only be useful for Leila, but also for herself, to put her thoughts, feelings and observations into words, she looked at me with amazement and a sense of relief. I added that I felt Leila needed to be reminded that she was missing her computer time.

Leila's worker explained that, because she was unable to make sense of what Leila was doing, she could not say anything until she understood. She herself seemed to be 'hiding', as if pretending not to be there either, as if then nobody would find out (not even herself) how 'incompetent' and 'stupid' she *felt* she was – a very common and 'normal' experience when with an autistic child, virtually the other side of the coin: the child takes no notice of you, so you feel rendered incompetent with nothing worth noticing to offer. But we can detach our ability to think, and to talk, from our sense of helplessness and meaninglessness created by the autistic state of mind. Although hard, it requires no more than keeping in mind that our ability to speak enables us to catch in words precisely this sense of bewilderment, our feelings, thoughts and observations – like butterflies in a net. All we have to do is get the net out.

Sometimes an activity may make sense to the child but not to the adult, as with Leila's marble activity, which had a sense of purpose about it, although what exactly that was, was not obvious to us. While I agreed with her worker's intuition that Leila's activity seemed different, it is important to remember that some repetitive activities are actually *meant* not to make sense. An autistic child's puzzling activity may make sense to both adult and child, to the child only but not the adult, only to the adult but not the child, or it may not make any sense at all, because it is intended to simply make time pass. The adult may feel that an activity is not good for the child's development, because he engages in it to eliminate all awareness of anything around him, such as Derek's jigging or Fred's wheel-twiddling. The meaning of Derek's jigging was to cut off and not notice anything – 'I am jigging so nothing matters.' But while Derek seemed to need this activity to be able to cope with the world, Fred seemed rather grateful when someone suggested to him that it was time he did something different. Having explained this, Leila's support worker found her words again. Talking to her seemed to wake Leila from some trance-like state and she greeted her worker's offer to use the computer with what seemed like relief.

There is something in some autistic children that seems to exert a deadly pull on the adult's mind into an apparently inescapable state of mindlessness. There is something catching, something contagious, in the way in which he does not respond to us, and it may feel pointless to talk to someone who seems not to even notice you, which is, of course, precisely the reason why we *should* make the heroic effort to speak to him, or otherwise encourage mental in-touchness. The last thing we want is to collude with his denial of our presence, his refusal to take notice of us as fellow human beings and the possibility of meaningful human contact. Not being able to get an ordinary response from a child may make us feel like a hopeless case ourselves: why are we unable to get through to this child and make contact, why can't we make sense of what is going on, why don't we understand? Putting exactly this into words can be a powerful way out of this hopeless helplessness dilemma. *Talk to him, if only because it keeps you alive and thinking.* As with a much younger child, it is a good idea to alternate between using 'you' and the child's name. Leila's support worker's commentary may have gone something like this:

> I am not sure what to do now, Leila. I thought you might like to play at the computer. ... [watching quietly] ... But I feel that you don't want to know that I am here with you. It's as if Leila is saying: 'No one here but

Leila – Leila and her marbles. Only Leila and her marbles here!' ... [watching quietly, then with some friendly urgency in her voice]: But I *can* see you: LEILA IS PLAYING A MARBLE GAME. I am not quite sure how it works. ... I am really sorry I don't understand. [Then thinking to herself]: *I feel I am no good, that there is nothing I can do to help her. It actually makes me feel quite useless and depressed.* [Acknowledging those feelings to herself allows her to let go of their paralysing effect and to return to Leila]: I can see that you are arranging your marbles in different patterns, this one and that one and another one. [Speaking in a larger-than-life manner]: Where is that one going? Oh, it's going over there with the big marbles. Lots of big ones. I think Leila says: where does the little one go? – Oh, that's where it goes, the little one goes over there, all by itself. ... [Then, in a more purposeful tone and with some urgency]: Listen, Leila, I think it's *time to do something different.* Time to put the marbles away. Play with the marbles again later: 'Bye bye marbles!' – let's play on the computer now! ...

It is possible that having described in detail exactly what Leila was doing, Leila's support worker may have understood a little more. But first she had to distance herself from her sense of inadequacy. Hearing oneself put one's feelings into words allows us to stand back and look at what is going on. Leila's worker may then have realised that, even without understanding the deeper meaning of Leila's marble arrangements, she was perfectly competent to describe what Leila was doing, and to return to her usual state of common sense to tell her when it is time to move on.

Describing in detail what he is doing is often a saving grace when feeling helpless and useless with an autistic child, because it reminds us of the power of our own mind and enables our own mental powers to function again. But it also builds communicative and emotional bridges between the child and us without putting pressure on him, so eventually he may be willing, even relieved, when we suggest doing something different. With Derek it usually went something like this:

I can see you really like jigging this toy.'Jig-jig-jig', says Derek. But I really don't like it. Watching it actually makes me feel sick – I don't think it's very good for you. ... Now you are jigging it a bit slower. Oh, running away! Derek ran away, and now he's come back again. There you are, Derek. [Said with a welcoming surprise]: Hello! – That was a nice little look: you looked at me. Yes, I am here watching you jigging that telephone. There are so many other things one can do with a telephone, but Derek just wants to jig it. 'Jig-jig-jig' says Derek. 'All I want to do is jig. Only Derek and the jigging. Nothing else.' But I can still see you ...

and I think it is time to do something different, Derek. I am getting really bored now. Aren't you bored? ... Come on, how about a jumping game? Derek likes jumping, : how about [gently but firmly taking his hands and guiding him] 'jump-jump-jump?' ...

The process of spelling out what one is seeing, feeling and thinking has life-saving potential for the adult. Allowing us to keep a grip on our own mind, it gives us something to hold on to, helping us sort out what we do or do not understand, whether there is anything to understand at all, what we may need to know in order to understand more, and how we could perhaps find out. It also helps the child to be aware that there is someone friendly there who is making an effort to understand. Even if Derek is shutting me out with all his might, chances are that some awareness of my commitment and attention does trickle through his cut-off-ness. And there is no way of knowing whether Leila was really not aware of her support worker's attention on her, or whether she just did not show it. The adult's mental effort of focussing on the child, of watching and describing, also acts as a model of how the child himself could focus his attention and use his own mind. He may hear, even if only now and again, when your words correspond with what he is doing, looking at, thinking or feeling. Hearing the words that correspond exactly to what a child is doing or experiencing is one of the most important building blocks in the development of early language skills ('shared attention'). Here is an example without a happy ending:

One day I saw Tim sitting on the floor next to a wooden dolls' pram, white paper-shreds scattered all around him, deeply absorbed in some purposeful activity, so unusual for him. I sat down to watch, then began to talk as if thinking out loud (and without expecting any response): 'What is it you are doing, Tim? ... I can see you are putting paper through the hole (i.e. the handle of the pram). ... All in: another one, and another one, ... all in. Do you like putting them *in*? Or are you making them fall *through*? ... You are picking them up very carefully. This one, and that one – and another one. ... Perhaps you are making them walk in circles like you do? ... What about this big tin? Do you want to put some in here too? No? I see. No, says Tim, not in that tin. What about this box? No? Maybe I was wrong. Maybe you are not putting them *in*. Are you making them fall *through*? What about this lid of a posting-box? Do you want to let some fall through this one? No? Is it too small, or the wrong thing? Am I wrong again? Or are you doing something different? ...'

Because I started off doing nothing more simple than to observe and describe what he was doing (or what I saw him as doing), I was able to formulate a little theory, and to think of ways to ask my developing questions. Wondering whether he was putting things 'in', something all young children are interested in, I expected him to be interested in putting his paper-bits into other containers too. The fact that he was not suggested that my initial assumption had been wrong. So I looked again at what he might be doing, and how he might be seeing things.

This is, by the way, an interesting example of how what we think of as no more than a perception is already an interpretation. I had thought that I was simply describing what I saw: that he was somehow putting things in. But I then realised that he was not putting things in at all, but was (perhaps) letting things fall through a hole – or something. The fact that I turned out to have been wrong made me feel that some real communication had taken place. Tim did seem to notice that I was watching him with interest, he accepted my 'action-questions' and 'answered' them by refusing my container offers, thus letting me know that he was on about something different. He was able to communicate and to correct me, although in indirect ways. We were having a conversation, only that he 'talked' with actions and rejections, which I could use to help me think, perhaps eventually to arrive at some understanding.

However, some people think that not only does the autistic child not understand language, but that one should not talk to him too much because it confuses him – and there certainly appear to be times when the autistic child does not understand. But how do we know? It seems to vary so much from child to child, from moment to moment, from week to week, as development goes on or not. Chances are that there is a whole spectrum of possibilities. The trouble is that we can never be sure whether he does, at this moment, understand or not, which raises the question whether it is better to err on the side of silence, underestimating his mental abilities to understand, hear and take in what we are saying, or of speaking too much, perhaps overestimating his mental capacities. But if talking keeps the adult's ability to use her common sense alive and functioning, if it enables her to think of ways of enlivening him and making some tenuous contact, then it may serve a purpose that is worthwhile and in the service of the child's mental growth and development.

Communication He Won't be Able to Resist: Make a Song and Dance of It!

Sitting next to a three-year-old, who seems to be staring holes into thin air in response to all our attempts to engage him into a human interactive encounter, can be soul-destroying. Walking alongside a silent four-year-old, who does not respond to any of our overtures, can drain the life out of the liveliest person, or make us go up in smoke with frustration. Making a conscious effort to give a simple running commentary is generally regarded as vital for speech development. A running commentary (which has nothing to do with running, as I had to explain to some carers) is a verbal descriptive commentary 'running along' – like a sports commentator on radio – just talking and describing what we see happening, what could happen, or what you or the child are or could be doing, feeling, thinking, or wanting. It helps the adult stay alive and thinking, reminds the child of the adult's friendly presence, and helps him structure his world, actions and thinking.

When a spoken running commentary is not enough, as often happens with the autistic child, he is usually reachable if we *sing*. People often think of singing only in terms of two or three familiar nursery rhymes. But singing does not have to be sitting down to sing a familiar routine of songs, although this is very useful too for encouraging the autistic child's communicative development. But singing can be used in a much wider sense: it is possible to sing your way through almost the entire day by *singing* your running commentary.

In our efforts to awaken in the autistic child an interest in social communication, we can probably find no better ally than music. Music speaks a purely emotional language that is primal and universal, and goes straight to our heart. The combination of the music's rhythm and tune affects us physically, it gets under one's skin and into one's bones, compels us to move in time with its rhythm and beat. It is almost impossible to resist the power of an Irish gig, a Samba, a Salsa, the rhythm of African drums. Their music reaches the listener directly and on a physical gut-level. A lively tune or rhythm will reach even the most cut-off child without making him feel invaded or threatened. Its message is directly meaningful without needing words, understood by listeners or music-makers of all cultures: the ideal medium for the autistic child who has such difficulties with meaning and words. Music can communicate and 'makes sense' without words – and is fun. Unlike speech and spoken words, it need not engage our rational mind, but can envelop us in the experience, as if safely wrapped up in a blanket or as if it is carrying us. The ongoingness and predictability of melody and rhythm can evoke a sense of security. The experience may also be of feeling full with music inside, or with M. Sendak, 'I'm in the song and the song's in me'.

The response to music is so elemental and physical as to be almost instinctive, and because sound is so inescapable, a musical tune or rhythm can cut right through the autistic child's isolation. It is not dependent on his motivation. Instead it seems to *create* motivation, even where there had been none before. As a magnet attracts metal filings into a tight tidy circle, the magnetism of music, of a musical tune or rhythm, pulls together one's senses into one integrated experience. The auditory stimulation continues as physical vibration throughout the body, uniting physical sensations with emotional feelings and mental alertness. Videos of Nordoff Robins Music Therapy demonstrate that musical communication almost invariably triggers a response which is immediate and almost instinctive, even in the most withdrawn and non-communicative autistic child.

A happy, lively tune can evoke interest or excitement and enliven a withdrawn child. To calm an overexcited or upset child, one will choose a quiet song or lullaby. Although singing and music can express a large number of different emotional states, it is virtually impossible to feel truly threatened or scared by a song or someone singing – a great advantage with those children who feel threatened easily and tend to cut off, run or turn away whenever someone approaches them.

The simplest and most natural human instrument is of course *our voice*. Not only is it always with us, but it is also the most sensitive, expressive and adaptable musical instrument, and it comes with the most exquisitely responsive visual display: *our face*. The human way of initiating one of our kind into the human art of vocal turn-taking and dialogue, those early pre-verbal, and mainly musical, skills without which no mastery of language is possible, is through those simple encounters when the sensitive and attuned parent uses his or her voice in melodic ways with a young baby.

We do not have to be musicians: it is not difficult to put whatever one wants to say into some simple tune, whether made up or borrowed from some familiar song. The tune of a song carries the words much as a mother, or push-chair, carry a baby, or a train carries people. The train goes on regardless of whether there are people in it or not. The push-chair can be pushed with or without a child, or with a doll, a coat or some bricks. You can do all sorts of things with it: put it away, get it out, turn it upside down, push it to and fro, knock it about, mess around with it. A tune too can be filled with words or not, sung to and fro, stopped and started, while staying itself. An empty train or push-chair is like a hummed or 'la-la-la' kind of song without words. The tune provides a musical container for any words or thoughts, such as running commentary songs using familiar tunes:

To get Ryan to stop running around when it is time to get ready to go out, we can use the tune of his favourite song 'Baa Baa Black Sheep' to sing
   'Come on, Ryan, we are going out.
   Put your shoes on and your coat'
(or socks or hat: there's no law that says things have to rhyme).
Instead of sitting silently with Patrick lining up play-people on the floor, we can sing to the tune of 'Here we go round the Mulberry Bush':
   1. 'Patrick's lying on the floor, on the floor, on the floor,
      Patrick's lying on the floor as he does every morning.'

2. 'Patrick's lining up the people, ...
   ... down here on the floo-or.'
Without interrupting his game, we can play with a tune to fit our words,
pointing to each of his play-people and sing:
3. '1 and 2 and 3 and 4, all together on the floor,
   5 and 6 and 7 and 8: Patrick's got all the people.'

Simply singing our running commentary, using either made-up bits of tunes
or rhythms, or the tunes of familiar songs with our own words to suit the
situation, can make an enormous difference. Every song has a typical
rhythm, a definite structure, so it can be repeated and recognised. The tune
envelops both in something akin to 'shared attention', enlivens the adult,
cheers up the child, jollies him along. It can even absorb frustrated feelings.
It needs no response to keep going, as it hangs together via the melody
whatever the words. It is almost as if a tune knows instinctively where it is
going, even if you don't: an excellent idea in all those dreadful times when
we feel so utterly stranded, lost at sea, with a non-responding autistic child.
The flow of the music simply takes singer and listener along, like water
down its riverbed. Interestingly, singing and flowing water have the same
attraction and soothing functions to many autistic children.

A made-up song can be exquisitely responsive to the child's facial expressions, vocalisations, movements or gestures, because the singer can observe
him, carefully pitching her singing accordingly. She can adapt, moment by
moment, to what she notices and feels is going on within the child she is
singing to – getting faster, or louder, or slowing down to gain momentum
again, if she feels she is losing his interest. Admittedly this may mean having
to overcome some reluctance to do something so 'silly' as using the tune of
'The Wheels on the Bus' to sing

'It is time to tidy up now, tidy up now, tidy up now,
it is time to tidy up now: the toys go in the box here.'

But it is worth a try. A later 'verse' may be

'Now it's time to wash our hands, ...
.... let's go to the bathroom!' or
'It is time for "Story-time", sit down Leila, Ryan too,
sit down Terry, sit down Max, everyone sit down now.'

This requires no great singing skills, and most adults have no difficulty
singing such familar tunes with any words that fit the situation. If you or

the child prefer a different tune, 'Old MacDonald' could be used just as easily, or any other.

Once a new song has been heard a few times, the listener expects it to continue after the first chords. If a familiar song stops prematurely, we feel compelled to finish it: a powerful tool to encourage communication and vocalisation in the autistic child. Try this:

Sing or hum a song and stop suddenly before it is finished, e.g.:
– 'Old McDonald had a farm, ee.',
– 'Wind the bobbin up, wind the.'
– 'Baa baa black sheep ha-.'

You might say you can't do it, that it does not make sense, that it doesn't feel right. And it doesn't. Just as you are bound to feel compelled to finish it, most autistic children will make a spontaneous sound to finish a familiar tune, provided the adult can wait long enough, tolerating the build-up of enough tension and suspense. Singing a familiar tune to a child, who is in a cut-off state causes him to be startled into alertness when it stops abruptly. The sudden, unexpected and perhaps ominous-feeling silence triggers surprise. He is grabbed by an urge to look up and see 'where is it?' He looks for clues of what happened, to where the sounds had been coming from: your face – a welcoming, friendly face with a broad smile. Often he will make a sound as if he cannot bear to leave the tune hanging in mid-air – the most simple, but most powerful tool to help the autistic child play the 'communication game' with us:

Sing a song he knows and likes – and suddenly stop, thus creating an expectant silence of suspense – and wait. Keep your attention focussed on him, encouraging him silently, with your eyes, to take up his cue to kick-start the tune into continuing: with a sound, glance, tiny silent nod, gesture, or whatever. Continue the song as soon as he has taken his turn in some way, like a song-conversation, or sing it again, or another one, rather than praising him: he did it for the music, not the praise – so keep singing. It is a good idea to have a shared sequence of songs which you both know and like, for example:
1. 'Wind the Bobbin Up'
2. 'Head, Shoulders, Knees and Toes'
3. 'I've got Ten Little Fingers'.
Once you have sung number 1, it is number 2, then number 3. In this way, he builds up an expectation of what is to come next, so he can then prompt *you*, if (and when) you get it wrong – so do give him that chance sometimes by 'forgetting' a word, a song, a line, or a verse.

Routines like a child's habitual 'bath song', lullaby or nursery rhyme serve the same function as the theme tune of TV programmes, ads, soaps or series. With the first jingles virtually every child, and the autistic child, come dashing to be in time for their favourite programme. It tells us that this is the beginning of a reliable sequence. It makes things predictable.

It is possible to take the singing even further, making almost everything into a 'song and dance', singing much of his daily chores and activities. The familiar tune not only acts as additional scaffolding for him to make sense of what is going on, or what he is expected to do. It also manages to gain his evanescent cooperation, as he feels compelled to finish or continue our song when we stop singing abruptly.

Although it helps to be musical, this is by no means necessary. The only thing needed is to want to convey a sense of fun and friendly companionship to the child. This can be done just as effectively by chanting or speaking in a rap manner, which relies on the predictable repetition of rhythm and beat, as songs do, but without the melody. It is of course also possible to create simple dialogue songs, initially taking both turns oneself.

> The familiar
> 'Rosy camel has three humps, three humps, three humps,
> Rosy camel has three humps. Go, Rosy, go! Boom boom boom ...
> Rosy camel has two humps, ...'
> can, for example, be made into
> 'Ryan can clap his hands, clap his hands, clap his hands,
> Ryan can clap his hands, what can Fatima do, boom boom boom?
> Fatima can flap her hands, flap her hands, flap her hands,
> Fatima can flap her hands – what can Jazzy do? Boom boom boom ...'

using Fatima's unintentional and stereotypical flapping as if it had been, or could be, a deliberate gesture or intentional communication. In this way the song is not interrupted, the singing can continue, and the autistic child is integrated in the singing time, whether she does or does not respond. For children who have difficulties with initiative, hearing the same song again and again, gives them a blueprint of what they might answer the next time the singer hesitates or pauses somewhere in the middle of the song.

Singing gets a response, it is a powerful instrument to reclaim the autistic child into our social world of communication. It can be a running commentary that keeps you alive and thinking. It can prompt the start of verbal communication as the child fills in the gaps when you pause expectantly, waiting for him to take his turn. Singing together, including pauses and silences, makes a duet. A duet is two players making music together. So who said the autistic child had no dialogue skills? Let's claim him into our song!

'It's Time to Do Something Different': Does He Know How, or Even That, He Could Stop?

That autistic children get themselves stuck in habitual or obsessive repetitive activities is well-known. With an autistic child around one is continually confronted with the question of how best to respond to his never-ending, never-changing self-absorbed activities, or non-activities: whether or not to allow him to continue, how to get him to stop, to do something more useful. The adult is dominated by a sense of insecurity. What should she do? It seems so boring, so pointless, so educationally empty. Yet the child clings to it so fiercely, gets so upset or desperate when stopped.

Tim spent his days walking around the room or garden in eternal eventless circles, or lying motionless in a corner, sucking on his T-shirt or some object. If someone stood in his way or line of vision, he simply walked around them or turned his head away, making the adult feel as if they did not exist.

Fred would sit staring at his fingers, a pen or small toy in an odd sort of way. If interrupted, he would walk away angrily to continue his strange activity.

Yusuf had been sitting by the sand all morning letting it trickle through his fingers. When his worker asked him to come to the toy library, he seemed not to hear her. When she took his hand, inviting him to come, he resisted her silently by making himself go solid and immovable.

Leila would insist with such tenacity and fierce screaming to be lifted into a swing as soon as she got to the playground, that adults felt they had no choice but to obey her (if only to stop the screaming). The battle of having to take her out was dreaded by all.

Terry often seemed like a wind-up toy gone wild in his constant frantic activity of running and moving and fiddling and causing havoc. Attempts at involving him in some other activity only seemed to make him more frantic, rushing around as if in a panic.

The adult may end up pushing Leila in the swing for hours, one as trance-like as the other, as if there was nothing else one could do. The adult may not even notice how bored she is herself. A frequent adult response to Tim's and Terry's constant and purposeless movement was to shut off themselves, to walk away and ignore it. Some people tried to comfort themselves that 'at least he is happy'. Others thought that, for some inexplicable reason, 'he *has* to do it', because of the nature of his disability, because he is autistic. But carefully watching the child's facial expression sometimes makes one wonder whether he really is relaxed and happy, whether a smile may in fact be more like a grin of helplessness, or something more unpleasant. There may be a strange quality to it like a forced attempt to stolidly (or sometimes triumphantly) keep going against all odds.

The child seems stuck in some meaningless and repetitive activity, without aim or purpose. So the adult tries to interest him in an alternative activity. This was easier with Fred: not only was his 'funny habit' of staring more bizarre, and therefore more noticeable to the adult, but he was also more willing to engage in another activity. The fact that he was sitting quietly made it much easier too to observe what he was doing, and to think about what would be good, or better, for his mental development. Often the adult's own thinking capacity is virtually wiped out, as by the onslaught of Leila's violent screaming, while Tim's and Terry's constant activity, and Yusuf's lack of it seemed to leave no space for any thought, their own or the adult's. Fred's 'funny looking' allowed for there to be a little bit of space for a thought, a new idea, for something new to happen, making his developmental prospects more hopeful.

Because of this paralysing effect on the adult's own mind, it rarely occurs to people that the autistic child may actually be stuck in his repetitive activity, unable to free himself without help. He may feel driven to keep going on and on by some invisible inner force which he is unable to control or put a stop to. It may be like being sucked into a whirlpool, like sinking in a bog with nothing to hold onto to stop the deadly suction and terrifying downward pull. He may have become so lost or absorbed in his repetitive hypnotic activity that he has lost all sense of time, with no idea whether he has been doing 'it' for a long time, a short time or any time at all. So, for lack of something better to do, he just carries on. In fact, he may not know *how* to stop – he may not even know or remember that he *could* stop. He may have great difficulty in accessing his own mind, and knowing how to tap into his own thoughts. He may not even know that he *has* a mind all of his own.

Even more fundamentally, the autistic child may not feel enough of a 'he' or 'she' to do any wanting. He may not have enough of a sense of himself to experience himself as someone who can want this or that, who can make choices and initiate getting what he wants. It is possible for an activity to take on its own momentum, so that the child comes to feel that it is the activity which is in control, that he has no power over it, that he is no more than a thing being spun, swung or driven into perpetual movement. Yusuf, Tim and Adrian sometimes seemed to be drifting like autumn leaves, aimlessly blown here or there by whatever wind happened to catch them from within. The autistic child sometimes seems to have become the object of some eerie force, like a satellite shot out of orbit circling round and round

– until its orbit is broken by the interference of some human 'satellite observer' on earth, summoning it back or redirecting its course.

Then, one day, someone suggested to me simply to point out to the child that he has got stuck with an activity, to suggest that he was bored – to remind him that he could stop, that he could do something different, and to draw his awareness to the point at which he gets bored or stuck (Klauber 1993). At first I did not think much of this. It seemed too abstract and complicated an idea for these young and unresponsive children to understand. It seemed too passive on my part, and expecting too much active mental processing from an autistic child. But I was going to give it an honest try: I had nothing to lose.

Next time Leila had been in the swing for what appeared like ages, and I was beginning to get bored (which made me wonder whether Leila too might be getting bored), I simply said to her, just as a piece of information: 'Leila, I think you are stuck. I think it's time to do something different.' Nothing much happened, and I did not really expect her to understand or respond anyway. I said it again, perhaps with more urgency. Then I waited – before following up my point by beginning to lift her out of the swing, repeating again that 'it's time to do something *different.*' I stressed the word 'different', so it stood out from the rest, but I also made sure to give it a friendly, coaxing, not a harsh and demanding feel. Usually, any attempt at lifting Leila out of the swing would have prompted murderous screaming and resistance (there had been times when two adults had been necessary to free the swing from the iron double-grip of this screaming, struggling three-year-old). Not this time – she simply let me lift her out of the swing and ran off to the climbing frame. It worked: there had been no battle – none for her, none for me. I was stunned. And I was going to try it again.

When I tried it again with other children, I became aware of the great sense of relief the autistic child might feel, if and when someone reminds him of the fact that he *could* stop, that there are other things he could do, that there is someone who is trying to help him locate the point at which an activity tips over from being interesting and enjoyable into the realm of being repetitive, obsessional, hypnotic, stuck, unstoppable and, essentially, dead and deadening. How exactly we help him depends, as always, on each child's individual personality. With some we have to be much more active, and it seems as if we have to do it for them, by taking them by the hand, engaging them in an interactive game or showing them something else they could do. Others latch on with great relief when someone helps them to notice the moment when they get lost and swallowed up in their 'funny ways', simply by pointing this out to them.

We may say something like '*I think you've got stuck*', '*That's not good for you*' or '*It's time to do something different*' – depending on child and situation, and in a tone of voice that is at the same time gentle, friendly, laid-back and expectant, perhaps even urgent. Then we must wait. Don't expect him to pack up immediately. Observe and be patient. But *do* expect him to understand something of what you are trying to tell him – if only the tone of urgency and expectation in your voice.

When Yusuf's key-worker was pulling silently at his hand, against his resistance, I suggested she insert one other step into her plan of action. Having explained the above, she sat down again by the sand-tray and said, with some urgency in her voice 'Yusuf, it's time to stop and go to the toy library.' She looked at me, and I motioned for her to sit back and wait. She did. There seemed to be no response from Yusuf. She looked at me again, and then repeated what she had said, this time with more expectant urgency in her voice, holding out her hand inviting him to come. He got up, took her hand and they went. As simple as that. She looked at me with amazement, unsure whether this was really happening. It was.

It does not matter whether he understands every word you are saying. It is *the message conveyed by your tone of voice, your eyes and posture* that counts, which means that you have some control over whether or not he understands, because you can 'make it bigger': you can make your voice sound more expectant and commanding of his attention. It may need some time to sink in, and you may need to repeat what you are saying with different intonation and tone of voice, more emphasis or less, more urgency, as much feeling as you can, and a lot of long, patient waiting. Give him time. Lots of it. You may need to point it out to him several times before he gets what you are on about – or that you are on about anything at all.

Don't muddy the water by being too active, talking too much, telling him to do something else. Make your comment, with the appropriately expectant urgency, and wait. You don't need to do much for a sense of suspense and expectation to build up. In fact, the less you do, the more it does. If you have created an expectant atmosphere but nothing is happening (because you are just waiting, without moving or speaking, just keeping your attention firmly focussed on him), it is as if you are almost 'willing' his mind and memory into gear. Almost invariably he will have to notice, to wonder, to wake up into some grating sense that 'something must be up'. He will have to look at you to find out.

Terry, constantly on the move, would whizz through the same repetitive routine with his toys every play session, tipping out toy boxes, running to and fro, flicking switches, jumping up and down, with a grin and gritted teeth, ... every time the same. It always set my head spinning. I was convinced when I first said to him 'Terry, that's not good for you. I think you're stuck. It's time to do something different', that my words would just get whizzed away like everything else, that he would not even hear it. But then I noticed a subtle change in his activity, and after a few days in which I continued trying, perhaps with little offers of alternative activities he could do, he put things away and moved to something else at the slightest suggestion of 'I think it's time to do something different.'

Terry seemed to be able to recognise that there was a moment in which he would drift off into an activity that he did not actually enjoy, which got hold of him with a fierce grip, and that I was trying to help him to gain some control over it.

All the Same or Different?:
On Pre-symbolic Mental Functioning

Autistic children do not play in imaginative ways; many do not speak, some use no words at all. They don't because they do not use symbols. But what are symbols? What is it that is missing? How is it different from the development of non-autistic children? We use symbols all the time without realising it, and we tend to take it for granted that everybody else knows how to do it too. But very young babies also do not use or understand symbols. Gradually they learn about the amazing human potential for symbolisation, and begin to play and use words.

Without symbols there can be neither play nor language. A symbol is something that stands for something else. In symbolic play a child will use a brick for a car or a house, a banana for a phone, a toy car and play-people *as if* they were real. She cannot move the actual furniture around in her house, she cannot drive her mother's actual car, but she can *pretend* that she is driving or doing other 'real' things. If I write 'car' or 'banana' or 'baby' I am using symbols, which enables you to think of these things without actually needing them here. A true symbol is also different from what it stands for: the words are nothing like a real car, banana or baby. They are at first just sounds which we come to associate with the meaning of what they stand for. Any word could be used as long as enough people agree on its meaning (which is what foreign languages are about). Usually a baby gets to this point of symbolic development naturally and in such a way that we fail to notice the amazingly complex developments leading up to it.

But in the autistic child, with his peculiar states of awareness, there are hitches in the process, and he tends to get stuck in the earliest stages of symbolisation. These are difficult for us to understand, because we are so used to being able to use language to organise our thinking. But it is possible to describe the pre-symbolic mental functioning as experienced by young babies and autistic children (as studied in infant observation courses (Bion 1962, 1967)). In order to be able to use and understand symbols, the child needs to feel separate from the outside world. One needs to be able to stand back enough from the car, banana or baby, to be able to see it in the first place, which is an enormous dilemma for all the as yet unconverted 'inside babies' (see chapter 7). The child who insists on being held will find it difficult to see and perceive his mum as the separate person she is. But without that little bit of distance, that allows us to see what something, or someone, looks like, we cannot see that there is someone there to talk to. And then – what would be the point of using symbols, to communicate, or talk?

We all know the baby game when this realisation first dawns on a child: it starts off with the baby trying to work out 'there' and 'gone' and how these two are connected. Well before their first birthday, babies can be seen playing their personal version of one particular game: they throw, push or roll something away, and retrieve it: 'gone!' and 'there again!' ...

At first the baby felt that something that was 'gone' was gone for ever. When Mummy left the room, it was a disaster: 'Mummy gone!' With no words yet to say it, he was beside himself with crying. When he began to crawl, he could find her again next door. What a relief: 'there!' But sometimes he could not find her, he could not see her. He cried for her, and screamed with those horrible frightened and angry feelings inside. He stopped, exhausted, and chucked his pull-along train out of his cot. Gone! He burst out crying again: now everything was gone! – But hey – shimmering through his tears, there's a red bead at the bottom of his cot-bars. What's that? He picks it up – and magically, his beloved train appears through the bars. It's come back! No – 'I *made* it come back!', he thinks, and he plays the 'gone! – there!' game for a long time. When Mummy returns, he chucks out his train and hauls it in: see?!

The next time she has to leave him, she is in for a surprise: none of the old upset baby. Instead he sits on the floor throwing his ball and retrieving it. 'Are you playing byebye-gone?', she says. He hugs his ball and smiles at her. She kisses him goodbye. 'I'll see you later then.' When he hears the door close, he throws and finds his ball. He knows he'll get her back.

Children's symbolic development follows a pattern of stages, whether autistic or not. It begins with recognising certain aspects that are important to him in various different things. At the very beginning the child, or baby, attends only to that quality he has singled out as important and ignores all the differences. Everything with this one quality is to him, to all intents and purposes, the same, for example hardness. Many autistic children seem to feel that hardness makes them feel safe. So anything that gives them this sensation of hardness makes them feel safe, whether car, cotton-reel, book, plastic toy, cup, pen, puzzle piece, or whatever: if it's hard, it's safe. The fact that to us all these objects are as different as could be, does not matter.

The baby in the above example was preoccupied with 'goneness'. To him his mother leaving felt 'sort of the same' as his train being gone. By hauling it back, he turned his passive experience of loss into an active one, which he could have control over. This is the first developmental stage towards using symbols. At first sight it looks similar to Fred's experience, though there's one major difference:

Fred found it very difficult to separate from his dad. He would scream and cling to him whenever Dad tried to leave. His key-worker had been dealing very sensitively with Fred's separation anxiety, making sure that she was always there to take over and introducing separations in tiny steps. She had allowed some setbacks, and then started all over again with settling him in, which had helped Fred to trust the process.

Then one day, the problem was solved: Fred sat on the floor tossing a small ball in the air, retrieving it, tossing, retrieving it ... When his dad, who had been talking to his key-worker, bent down to kiss him goodbye, Fred did not look up but muttered a casual 'byebye' without interrupting his ball-play in any way, and Dad left without upset. 'He said "byebye"!'– it seemed unbelievable. Fred had never said a word before.

The big difference between Fred's play and that of the above baby is that the baby wanted to share his discovery with his mother, and did so success-fully. Fred did not. When he played 'gone – come back', his father did not seem to matter any more. He could go. It was not obvious at first, but over time it became clear that Fred was not playing with his little ball to explore and learn about the properties of absentable objects. He did not, like the baby, play this game in order to develop structures in his mind that would help him make the emotional challenge of Dad being gone more bearable.

What had started off as a promising attempt at early symbolisation, turned out not to be driven by the open question of 'What can I do with this?', but by a closed insistence that 'I don't mind about Daddy going, because I have control over come-back and gone-ness. He isn't gone at all,

I have him in my hand in the form of a solid red ball.' This, he felt, was a much better way of dealing with his pain over Daddy's leaving, because it erased his pain as with a rubber, with none left to suffer. But with this he also threw away his father's humanity, his awareness of his father's ability to feel for Fred, to miss and to think of him in his absence.

This early use of something as a substitute for something else is called a 'symbolic equation', because certain objects are equated and experienced as if they were the same. The differences are ignored. Anything will do for 'there! – and – gone!': trains, balls, spoons, teddies, daddies, can all give him the same feeling or sensation. Autistic children tend to get stuck at this stage, where objects can be replaced by one another without any objection. He may even accept it with relief.

Leila had the most awful screaming attacks for months when finally being weaned from her bottle. She frantically tried to suck the buttons on people's clothes (even strangers' on the bus), the knob on the lids of teapots, the round nut holding the wall mirror, a raised mole on my cheek. When a posting-box was offered to her as a substitute, she put shapes into their holes with great relief, and her screaming attacks stopped (see chapter 6).

The principle of 'symbolic equation' affects almost everything autistic children do. Some conform to the very basic principles of the earliest human baby preoccupations, others are more ideosyncratic. Some typical 'symbolic equations' are:

- bottle-teat = nipple of breast = knob of teapot lid = piggy's nose = clothes button = bell button = cotton-reel = mole on my cheek = finger = posting-shape = knot of trouser-cord = *something small and round that is sticking out and can be sucked to produce comforting feeling*
- posting-box = letter-box = video recorder = washing machine = drawer = oven = stomach = car = cupboard = *he can put things inside and make them be 'gone' – and 'there' again when he wants to*
- dinner = sand = play-dough = paint = flour = glue = water = biscuit softened in mouth = *creates skin sensation, can be handled, squished, mixed up and eaten*
- mouth = bin = plug-hole = toilet = window = doors = *hole through which he can make things disappear*
- hoover = dog = washing machine = rubbish-chute = *swallows things up with loud 'gobbling-up' noises*

What further drives a child's development of symbolisation is his motivation to share his experiences, especially of difference and of what is *not* there. In order to be able to communicate or talk about something which is absent or missing, one needs to be able to bear the frustration of things being gone, at least to some extent (= frustration tolerance), which is so difficult for autistic children. But once some degree of symbolisation is mastered, the child is no longer at the mercy of uncontrollable waves of raw sensations.

We can help the autistic child tremendously by encouraging him to differentiate, to be aware of differences by naming these for him. This way he may be able to gain some control over the world, by thinking about things and their differences, rather than equating them and denying their differences. By pointing out the most common differences over and over, things may become more manageable and digestible, thus losing their all-absorbingness for the autistic child. The preoccupations of young children are about familiar differentiations:

there–gone   in–out   inside–outside up–down   on–off
hard–soft   full–empty big–little   light–dark nice–nasty/scary
rough–smooth clean–dirty intact–broken loud–soft hot–cold

By being alert to what may be preoccupying the young autistic child, we can help him sort out where his activities are likely to support his growth into human company and interaction, and where they are blocking such humanness. Being able to tolerate differences is the key. This does not need to be as painful and unbearable as the autistic child is prone to believe. When we offered Leila the posting-box to replace her bottle, she was grateful: the shapes fitted as comfortably as the bottle had fitted into her screaming mouth. To help Fred with his separation anxieties, his key-worker played 'gone! – there!' games whenever she could with his car or other toys, or all sorts of versions of hide-and-seek. With every child we can watch out for those fundamental differentiations, naming them for him whenever possible. By joining in with open-hearted interest in his activities, keeping some of the above principles in mind, we can introduce, drip by drip, some awareness of differences and things being *not* the same, or of being the same in different ways, and that being O.K.

3
Dangerous Holes and the
Importance of Feeling Contained

'He Won't Take his Coat Off':
Feeling Contained: Coats, Covers and Inside Spaces

Some young autistic children appear to be extremely sensitive, fragile and raw, as if lacking a protective skin to hold them together. They may want to be picked up all the time, clinging blindly to any adult. Others appear to be utterly lost, unable to settle to any activity. But although holding him may stop the crying, it also stops his mind from being available for looking, learning and being curious about the world.

> Starting nursery was an upsetting experience for Tim and everybody else. Separating from his mother was not so difficult, because as soon as she had sat him in his seat on the school bus, he was quiet again. What made him fall apart was having to get out of his seat, out of the bus and walk up the stairs. By the time the nursery day began, Tim was crying pitifully and as if utterly lost. Every day for over seven months, he only calmed down if an adult picked him up to carry him around.

Adults often feel desperate about what to do, and console themselves that 'He'll stop, once he's settled.' But six months later, he still hasn't settled, seems as lost and raw, crying inconsolably.

As long as he was passed from his mother's arms into a containing seat or a buggy, Tim did not mind leaving his mum. It seemed as if in this way he was able to wipe out the experience of separation, as if there had not been one. But having to walk up the stairs was just too much, too much separateness for him to tolerate. We discovered how much it helped Tim (and everyone else: his crying was painful to bear), if we *carried* him upstairs from the bus. It helped him make the transition away from Mum, and out of bus and seat, more easily and without causing him (and us) quite so much distress. But, not only was he heavy and carrying him made it difficult for that person to attend to other children – it did not seem to have really helped Tim so far. It had not helped him build up a sense of feeling safely held within his own skin, able to go off by himself to explore and play. Although it made him stop crying, being carried seemed to have become more of an addiction, and hard work for the adult without fostering healthy mental development in Tim, who would hang on the adult's arm without looking or taking an interest in anything. How can we help the autistic child, insisting on remaining an 'Inside Baby' (chapter 7)? If we pick him up, he'll merge into the sensation of being held, he'll shut off his mind and eyes – if we put him down, he collapses into heartbreaking and inconsolable crying, until we pick him up again, in an apparently never-ending vicious circle.

Seeking to feel contained securely, Tim was not unlike the six-month-old who wants to be carried or to sit supported by a cushion when awake. Normally the four-year-old has long moved on and has become able to contain himself, at least for some of the time. When not too overwhelmed by upset or anxiety, he feels contained enough within his own skin. This allows him to concentrate, which in turn provides him with a further sense of containment. The autistic child, however, has become caught in a vicious circle, unable to contain himself, to hold himself together. Tim was one of these 'skinless' children. He had not developed a sense of his own skin and body-boundary that gives us a feeling of where we begin and end. It rarely occurs to us that walking from one room into another, or changing from one acitivity to another, could be a problem. But already the idea of it seemed to make Tim fall apart.

When he wasn't being carried, Tim seemed to recreate this experience by limply lying somewhere. If he was not crying and grizzling, he would be staring into space, his eyes at half-mast, sucking the string of his track-suit bottoms (how often I wished his mum would replace them with an elastic). Initially, we tried again and again to interest him in toys, games or activities. But if this meant having to get up and walk over to a table, he would simply go limp and cry. If toys or books were brought to him, he would turn his head away or close his eyes. Sitting by him talking or singing to him also did not comfort him when in this state.

Most of us remember moments when we ourselves felt unbearably raw and vulnerable, insecure and as if skinless, with a gaping heart and desperate for someone to take us into their arms or put their arm gently around us. Often some gentle words or a warm look can fulfil the same function. When our own mind alone is not enough, we need the help of another person's containing mind. But with the autistic child this is a problem.

Eventually we found that putting a blanket around him helped. Tim would pull it up to his chin, calm down and relax. This was great progress: using his own initiative and his own mind to think at least a little, perhaps 'Oh, a cover! Can I can pull it up? Yes.' In this way, Tim became more aware of being able to make himself feel better. Soon this could be extended into gentle peekaboo games with this blanket (*without* taking it away from him) to catch his attention.

We then began to bring a blanket (or large towel) down to the bus to wrap around Tim when he arrived in the morning, before taking him upstairs where he could now be happily put down. Whenever he got upset, we put a blanket or towel around his shoulders. Getting out of the bus, even walking upstairs and settling into a new day at nursery, ceased to be a traumatic experience. Through the repeated experience of feeling contained in such tangible ways Tim developed a little more of his own sense of skin.

Comforting a young child who is upset and crying by putting a small blanket around him often works. Anything that gives him the protective feeling of having a second skin will do: a towel, someone's cardigan, a jumper. The child feels that someone cares about him, providing him with the means to comfort himself, thus returning to him some control over his own feelings of lostness, hurt and despair.

Weaning a child off such a protective layer needs sensitivity and consideration. Some children cling to their coat or jumper, regardless of whether it is much too hot or socially unacceptable, such as wearing a winter coat indoors. Understanding this as the young child's way of saying 'I feel insecure, as if I will fall apart if I take this off' helps us to think of ways to help him develop his confidence, and a more secure sense of himself.

Harvey's mother was angry because his workers could not get him to take off his coat at nursery: why did they not treat him the same as the other children? *They* did not keep their coats on! And she showed the nursery staff how to do it: sternly she pulled it off herself, undeterred by his crying and resistance. This done, she left. But Harvey seemed to feel so raw and lost. And he did not learn. Every morning the same scene.

Harvey needed smaller steps towards taking off his protective layer. Perhaps his worker could have suggested to Mum to send in a 'nursery cardigan' for him to change into in exchange for his coat – in this way meeting both Harvey's extreme vulnerability and his mother's wish for socially acceptable behaviour. But above all, it would have helped Harvey to develop a mental sense of containment, as he would then be able to think about his 'nursery cardy', i.e. he then could have asked for it, should anyone forget. A sensitive and thoughtful response like this helps the autistic child develop mental structures for a less anti-developmental, and more healthy, attitude towards the outside world.

The principle of providing a child who is in some way lost or unsettled with a means of containment can be adapted to many other contexts and situations. Especially the young autistic child who tries to deal with his sense of feeling lost in more active ways by running around, can often be helped to settle in a small cozy containing space that 'just fits':

Wherever he went, Yusuf would find a small space or corner in which to sit. A toy car to sit in would be his first choice. But the activity cube, the doll's pram, a cardboard box would do just as well.

The only time Ryan would stop running around to sit and focus on something, was when in the toy car. Then he was able to do a posting-box, look at a book, sing some songs with his worker.

A car they can sit in is such a favourite with young children because it makes them feel contained. But I have also seen a high-backed potty-chair, a sturdy dolls' pram, an enclosed baby-swing, a small chair with arms used successfully to provide a child with such a sense of containment. Sometimes, a buggy can fulfil the same function – although some people complain that one should not encourage a three- or four-year-old to sit in a buggy indoors. Admittedly having a four-year-old sit indoors in his buggy is somewhat unusual. But if it provides him with a secure base into which he can snuggle, when feeling raw and miserable, and from which to begin to look around – perhaps even joining in with our singing group (or at least not disrupting it for all the other children with his running around and his insistence on doing whatever he wants) then: why on earth not?

The great advantage of a confined safe space for such a child is that it leaves the adult free to sit near to engage with him in simple communicative games, like 'Mouth and Face Games' (chapter 5), singing action-songs, or even looking at books together. With some children this is impossible because as soon as they are on your lap or arm, they merge with you, switching off mentally. Or they cling to you so tightly that there is no space in which you could show them something or even take up a face-to-face position. But when the physical holding and containment is provided by a buggy, a swing, a cardboard box, it is much easier to sit facing him, to attract his attention, to try to interest him in a toy, a book, your face, or an interactive game.

His Daily TV and Video Bath:
How Much Is Good For Him?

We have become a video and TV culture, and many people spend hours 'in front of the box'. Everyone does. The autistic child wanting to watch TV all day seems to be just like any other three-year-old. Parents often see this with relief. Surely, he too will learn something from watching TV and videos? But then doubts begin to creep in. He never talks about it. It does not seem to affect him. He does not play-act what he has seen like his age-mates. He only wants to see the one video again and again. On closer inspection, it actually looks like some kind of addiction.

> Harvey wants to watch the same video every day. He screams until his parents can bear it no longer and give in. It's been the same video for months now. 'At least it keeps him quiet', they explain – which allows them to get on with their daily chores.
>
> Tim does not seem to mind what he is watching as long as the TV is on. Lolling somewhere on the floor or settee, chewing on his T-shirt, he appears to be asleep, were it not for his eyes, which are open, but do not follow any movements on the screen.

Because of the autistic child's difficulties with communication and making sense of perceptions, his experience of what goes on in a film is likely to be very different from ours. If he lets his mind fall apart or is unable to pull his senses together into one single meaningful focus, then whatever he is watching will not make sense. If it does not make sense, then we are faced with the serious question: what is he getting out of this passive 'activity'.

It is a good idea to watch carefully what the child *seems* to be looking at on the screen, and whether this is accompanied by any changes of expression on his face in line with the story. Although the changes are subtle, it is possible, to a certain extent, to see on a person's face, and from other bodily reactions, whether they are following and understanding a story or not. Mothers and teachers do this all the time when telling a story or looking at books with children. With some practice it becomes increasingly possible to tell the difference between someone whose eyes simply follow the movement that is going on in front of them, and the person whose eyes follow movement and focus on the main aspect of the story for as long as is appropriate to the story. This person gives other signs too of emotional involvement with the characters: being upset, excited or happy in response to the characters – often lacking in the autistic child.

Making sense of the story-line in a film, although so immediate and natural to you and me, is really a complicated mental process, which is impossible without a good grasp of language and comprehension. Essentially it requires the ability and the desire to make sense of things, to understand what things 'mean' and to let them affect us – the autistic child's blind spots. But what is left of the TV or video experience, if we take away the story-line and the meaning of what is said and shown on the screen? A purely sensuous sight–sound experience, a 'sight-and-sound bath': a constantly changing colourful display of movement with an ongoing background noise of patterns of sound, or tunes.

To help us understand and think of the best ways of dealing with the child's TV addiction, a useful exercise is to experiment in watching TV without attention to the story or what the programme is about:

> With the TV on, focus your eyes into the far distance, so that your vison becomes blurred and your awareness dispersed. Focus your attention instead on the *patterns* of movement on the screen and let these drift past you without trying to make sense of them or matching them to what is going on in the story. It is possible to listen to the patterns of sound without listening to the meaning of the words, just letting yourself be carried away by the ongoingness of the rhythms and the music of the sound patterns. Letting the world go by in this way, as if nothing to do with you, creates a timeless experience – bathing in the sensations of sight and sound, a 'video-shower'.

But without meaningful seeing, there will be little learning. Most young autistic children do not learn much from watching TV or video. They use the 'sight–sound bath' to envelop, to wash over them in a comforting way, allowing them to cut off, to let themselves drift off passively. Surrendering to that sensual and essentially mindless experience means that much of their mental functioning is switched off, with brain activity, and learning, probably on standby. Periodically, his attention is activated by the catchy attention-grabbing jingle of advertisements, before ebbing off again into the more soothing, or hypnotic, lullaby-like flow of sounds.

The autistic child needs our help to make his TV watching into an edu-cationally valuable experience. Perhaps he can learn that there are other ways of watching TV than the way *he* does it? Perhaps we can show him that other ways of watching TV are fun, perhaps even more enjoyable than his habitual 'sight–sound bath'? Bearing in mind his developmental level, i.e. that we are watching TV with someone with a mental age of less than one, we may sit with him and describe and name some things we are seeing, in order to focus his attention. Such 'running commentary' has to be very simple, initially focussing mainly on movement, sudden surprising movements especially, which attract attention by their suddenness alone.

We may say a surprised 'Uh! It jumped!' or a dramatic 'Gone!' when something disappears from the screen, and then 'there it is!' Whether this 'something' is a person, a dog or a thing, the main character or the end of the film, is irrelevant to any child at this early developmental stage. It helps to point out all those 'things' that would be of interest to a baby, i.e. basic concepts such as 'there – gone', 'hello – byebye', 'in – out', 'up – down', 'round and round', and so on. We want to keep claiming his attention to help him focus his senses on one main event which you can both see, hear and share. It also helps to make links with other things you know he knows, just as one would with a one-year-old (and in the same 'baby language'): 'It's gone "bye bye" – just like Daddy this morning.' or 'Look! He's eating cornflakes! Harvey likes cornflakes. "Yum yum cornflakes," says Harvey.' Sometimes we can also make links with nursery rhymes the child knows, adding a bit of song to our joint TV session.

A huge amount of thoughtful and one-sided effort is required from the adult with the aim of establishing 'shared attention' in an experience that is shared between adult and child. By making his experience into a shared and interactive one, the adult can inject moments of meaningfulness into the autistic child's sensuous experience.

However, what has been said so far does not address another important function of TVs and videos in a busy family: that of a reliable, cheap babysitter, giving an exhausted mother a few minutes respite, in which to do something for herself, which is so important. But the danger is to *overuse* this 'babysitter' – as it may reinforce exactly the kinds of anti-communicative habits we so want the child to overcome. If sitting in front of the TV means he practises precisely those mental habits of cutting-off and going vacant that we are trying to discourage, then we are sawing the very branch we are sitting on. Using this kind of cheap babysitting service may cost us dearly, if it means that he practises his autistic sensual states of mind daily to further perfection.

Billy had spent most of his babyhood in front of the TV. His mother had spent little time playing with her easy-going baby and Billy never complained about being left alone with the TV. It was almost as if the TV was his mummy, always there, always talking to him, making him feel contained with its sights and sounds. When he later learnt to speak, aged six, he spent most of his day reciting bits from videos or TV, as if his inner world was made up of video images.

In some ways, the TV reflects precisely what the autistic child thinks of life and communication: a barrage of sensory stimulations, of sights and sounds, that have nothing to do with him, do not affect him, go on entirely according to their own agenda, without regard for what he is doing and feeling. In this sense it is as if 'the box' is just as uncommunicative (and autistic?) as the autistic child: neither engages in a dialogue with the world around them, both are unresponsive and expect no responsiveness from their environment (including interactive TV). A video can be seen as just as echolalic as the echolalic autistic child, echoing fragments of text and undigested, indigestible, bits of language. Both need a thoughtful, alert person to make sense of what goes on. The autistic child needs the help of a sensitive adult, who can inject moments of meaningfulness, and regulate the amount and quality of TV he watches.

'Put It in The Bin':
The Relief of Knowing a Place for the Bad Stuff

With some autistic children any occasion of food and eating turns into a nightmare for everyone, because of their apparently unstoppable urge to suddenly chuck food or utensils into the room. Throwing, especially of food during mealtimes, is one of those behaviours that can infuriate adults, often leading to angry scenes, and that do not respond well to behaviour modification, partly because it happens so suddenly that all the adult can do is mop up the mess, and shout and grumble.

> During dinnertime Jazzy would throw bits of food with vehemence, and all of a sudden, which greatly exasperated his carers. Telling him not to do it had absolutely no effect. Each time his key-worker scolded him with 'no's' and 'Don't do that!', making him pick up what he had thrown, in the hope that this would 'teach him'. It never did. Each time he would simply throw again what he was made to pick up, with further angry scolding. While being dragged to where it had landed, Jazzy would invariably snatch some food from other children's plates, either to eat or throw. He would wriggle out of her hold, run away into some corner where she could not reach him, or around the room with her chasing after him. To the uninvolved observer it was an unbearable experience – or a bad joke. To Jazzy it was clearly a welcome game of tease. His key-worker dreaded mealtimes.

Socially unacceptable in our day and age, this kind of throwing belongs in the category of the 'get rid of it' behaviours, which are characterised by a strong centrifugal force sucking all mental capacities in its vicinity into its deadly spin. Jazzy and his key-worker were of course most directly affected, but everyone else in the room (or anyone who met with either of them shortly afterwards) was also affected by their ordeal. With this approach, Jazzy never learnt how to deal with whatever his problem was in a different way, nor did his key-worker. The sense of overall helplessness and frustration was heart-breaking.

In order to resist the force that spins our adult mental functioning out of existence together with the child's, we need to sit back to watch carefully what may be going on for the child. Then it is sometimes possible to find surprisingly simple solutions. It was when we held back our urge to stop his socially unacceptable behaviour that we managed to solve Jazzy's problem. We held back to allow us to observe carefully *how* he did what he was doing, and to try to *understand the meaning of this behaviour for him and from his perspective.*

Jazzy had always been a fussy eater. But after some months at the nursery, chips and bread had become his favourites and he was now able to sit at the table, rather than chasing around the room. One day he had eaten all his chips, and bitten the soft part out of several quarters of bread, leaving only a few bits of crust – when suddenly one of those came flying across the room. Then another.

The bread crusts seemed to bother him very much when on his plate, and Jazzy got rid of them with force in the most concrete way of 'out of sight, out of mind'. It was also obvious that the usual suggestion to put unwanted bits of food on the side of one's plate was unbearable for Jazzy – and indeed to most small children, who feel that what they don't want is bad, and that the 'bad stuff' must be kept far away from their 'good food': if the 'bad stuff' shares the same plate as the 'good stuff', they might touch or get mixed up, and then the bad will contaminate the good and make it all go bad. Jazzy seemed to consider certain foods bad and uneatable. In order to make room for more of what he considered to be 'good food' (bread with the soft inside or chips), he had to clean his plate of 'bad' bits. So he chucked them.

We all know moments when we refuse to finish a bowl of delicious soup after finding a hair in it, even though the hair has only been in contact with a little part of the soup and could easily be lifted out (as if hair were that contaminating! It may have been our own, just washed). But the sense of disgust, of revulsion, is enormous. Most of us will decline, often vehemently, to continue eating the 'dirty soup', or even to use the same bowl. Many people will refuse to eat an apple, or a piece of cake, that has been bitten by another person, saying that it is disgusting. On the other hand, mothers especially, often finish the food started by their own children, rather than throw it away. They may complain that it is cold, or too mashed up, or even 'disgusting', but they would rather eat it than put it in the bin: just like Jazzy eating things off the floor in a way which I have come to call 'hoovering', another form of 'get rid of it'.

Observing Jazzy it was obvious that the act of throwing, that vehement gesture of hurling it away, was important: the vehemence of his action seemed to express the intensity of his feelings. I then wondered where he could possibly throw this terribly bad unwanted stuff with as much vehemence as he felt it needed without offending what we consider to be 'socially acceptable': perhaps a container with some depth might do, so that what needed to be got rid of could be hurled *into* it, and out of sight – which to a child's mind may feel safer than having the 'bad stuff' simply and visibly *on* a plate (where it may fall off, slide down, get mixed up). We are all familiar with this, from stuffing that most unwanted Christmas present into the back of our cupboard, rather than leaving it lying around, because we can't bear the sight of it. I also thought of young children's particular liking of posting-boxes and 'there-and-gone' games.

I therefore reached for the bin, placed it firmly next to Jazzy, took one of his discarded bread crusts and thrashed it with exaggerated pretend-vehemence into the bin saying an equally exaggerated '*In! – AWAY! – Into* the bin – *Bin!*' Jazzy was fascinated – and stopped. He seemed to recognise his feelings in my action, and copied me with another crust, thrashing it into the bin. I encouraged him, and, he threw the other bits from his plate in too. I explained '*Not* on the *floor*. Into the *bin! – Away! – In!*' He called out 'for!' several times, very communicatively. I knew that he knew his numbers and my mind was racing: 'four? 4? for?...?' He said it again and again, clearly trying to tell me something, but I just didn't understand. Maybe he was also straining to get up, so I said 'Show me.' He dashed to two chips on the floor: 'For!', he called. 'There are chips on the *floor!*' I summed up, delighted to understand. One of those chips immediately landed in his mouth. With the other he ran to fling it into the bin chirping '(A)*way! – Bin!*' My heart lept with joy.

Jazzy seemed to have quite a good sense of there being good and bad things in the world. Of those two chips on the floor, one was good and for him to eat, the other bad and for the bin. The following weeks proved that, within no more than a few minutes, Jazzy's favourite dinner-time game (and the one most dreaded by his key-worker) had been transformed: the unbearable scenes of being told off and chased around the room for the unacceptable throwing of food, resistant to previous attempts at behaviour modification, had changed to the delight of using the bin for unwanted stuff in the most socially acceptable manner. Not only that, but within these few minutes, Jazzy had also learnt at least three new words and concepts, together with a delighted and relieved way of solving what, in truth, was much more *his* than *our* problem. I am fairly sure that he only discovered the words for 'floor' and 'bin' just then, as he had never previously been heard to say them, and because of his delight when saying them. The word and idea of 'away!' also seemed to fascinate him (as they would any young child).

When dinner was finished, I asked him to take dishes, plates, cups, etc. to the hatch, but to put empty yoghurt pots, tissues and other rubbish into the bin. Jazzy wasn't one for being cooperative. But he complied with great keenness with my request to 'put it in the bin'. I showed him which was to go where, then handed him one item at a time, telling him whether to put it in the bin or in the hatch, pointing with my eyes only. Soon I simply expected him to know what went where when handing it to him. And he did! From then on, he loved the new 'game' of putting unwanted things into the bin. He knew where the bin was in each room, and what it was for, and he seemed so proud when asked to help, when expected to be able to do such an important task as putting tissues, dirty nappies, an empty wrapper, a broken pen into the bin.

I have found the same relieved response with many of the more active autistic children, when told about the bin, and when given the responsibility to use it to differentiate the bad from the good stuff. Most would never respond to the request to put something onto the table or to give it to someone. But when asked to find and put a dirty tissue or nappy, an empty yoghurt pot, banana skin or biscuit wrapper into the bin, they know exactly what is required, what the bin is for, and where to find it (having perhaps had it pointed out just once) – and they are delighted to get rid of this rubbish into its rightful place. For Jazzy, and all the other children, it was a great relief to realise that rubbish could be clearly differentiated from good stuff, that there was a definite place for it, to prevent it from messing up the good stuff, and that he had some control over this himself. Being given the trust, the credit and the responsibility that he could do it by himself, made him feel important and in control, thus curbing his franticness.

For the development of the child's sense of self, it is most important we hold back from doing these little tasks ourselves. Some adults seem to confuse helping with doing everything *for* the child. Instead of allowing him his little sense of pride and self-importance, they seem unable to resist the urge to take the rubbish from his hand to put into the bin themselves. But this deprives him of an important experience. To us putting something in the bin is an unimportant (even disgusting) act not worth mentioning. But to any young, and the autistic, child it is a hugely important experience to realise that he can himself differentiate good from bad stuff, that the bad stuff has a safe place into which it can safely be banished, and, above all, that *he* can do it. In this way we help him to develop his sense of self and independence.

'Get Rid of It!': On Throwing, Screaming, Eating Dirt and Running Away

Some of the most irritating behaviours, which frequently drive carers up the wall, appear to have nothing else in common except for their infuriating resistance to attempts at behaviour management. Some children have screaming attacks or throw tantrums that seem to go on for ever. Others hurl something across the room with the most startling suddenness, perhaps even most precisely aimed at another person or child. Some throw food in a similarly unexpected way during mealtimes, or squash, smear and spread it all over table, clothes and other people. Others seem to have the sudden compulsion, time and again, to tip over their cup, spilling juice all over the place. Some tip out every container of toys, or swipe everything off tables and onto the floor. Some seem compelled to bite their nails, bits off any toys, to eat the dirt from under their shoes, or anything that is on the floor, whether indoors or out, including paper, dirty tissues, old chewing-gum, bits of fluff or foods they would never eat from their plate. Some seem continually preoccupied with wanting to run away.

Many of these behaviours are dangerous, some simply maddening – all are socially unacceptable, leaving the adults at their wits' end. On the surface they all look totally different. But careful observation, combined with an understanding of how the mind of the young pre-verbal child works, suggest that all these distressing and irritating behaviours might actually be about the same thing. If we could understand what motivates the autistic child to behave in these perplexing ways, then we could perhaps respond in ways that are helpful to him, and to us, rather than fighting like Don Quixote against incomprehensible windmills. In fact, all these infuriating behaviours seem to be attempts to get rid of or away from something:

> Max kept throwing his ball, he struggled or ran away, climbed without looking and without any fear that he might fall and hurt himself. He screamed to get rid of unwanted adult interference. At other times, he 'plugged himself up' with his bottle, letting his mind go blank and his eyes drift into the 'unseeing distance'.
>
> Jazzy got rid of any 'sticking-out-bits' on toys or objects, including any sharp bits on his fingernails, by biting them off. He got rid of unwanted food by chucking it into the room (later into the bin).

Adrian ran and ran, as if driven by nothing but the idea of wanting to get away, with no space to think about any dangers, fears or anxieties. He often also 'got away' simply by falling asleep.

Leila's incessant piercing screaming made everyone's mind go dead. There seemed to be nothing anybody could do to help, because all thinking capacities that could have been used to find ways of helping her were blasted out of action by her mind-shattering screaming.

Driven by a most urgent need to get rid of whatever bothers him psychologically in a very concrete, immediate and direct way, whether actual things, toys or objects, or because he is suddenly overcome by a wave of feeling frustrated or lonely or frightened, the autistic child's response is immediate and he throws, bites off, swallows whatever is right in front of and bothering him. He runs away or screams, so his mind is full of loud noise, deadening all unwanted awareness. Too many toys on the table, unwanted food on the plate, bits that shouldn't be on the floor, may 'spoil' the clean appearance or surface, and bother his eye. What I call 'hoovering', i.e. eating anything that happens to be on the floor, whether food or not, might be the attempt to get rid of this disturbance by making it be 'gone'. In fact, a key characteristic of the autistic child's mental functioning is this way of instantly getting rid of and wiping out anything he finds troublesome, anything demanding a thoughtful response.

Max arrives at playgroup appearing lost. He wanders around, grabs the odd toy, throws it. He wriggles away from any attempts at involving him to play with a toy, in order to climb on the cupboard. Standing on a wobbly pile of books for height, he is about to climb on top of the gerbil cage. I lift him down, telling him gently but firmly 'No climbing, Max!' He screams, walks off, swishing toys off a table, and climbs onto the drawing table. I tell him not to and lift him off. After several repeats I explain 'This is climbing, Max. There's no climbing! You need to come down', thinking that perhaps he may not understand what is meant by 'no', by 'climbing' and by 'no climbing'. He slips on some paper, but catches himself so as not to fall. A box of pencils goes flying everywhere. I lift him down again with 'No climbing, Max.' When I turn round, he has climbed onto the cupboard again and is about to stand on the gerbil cage, (and so on) ...

A water-tray is set out for him. He is no longer allowed to play with the taps as he has flooded the bathroom so many times. He fills up a play-beaker and puts it to his mouth so water flows both into his mouth and down his face and onto the floor, again and again. I show him about pouring, but he shrugs off any interference angrily and successfully to continue drinking and spilling the water. The beaker is taken away to allow him to use his hands to play with the water. He grabs another one, with more water pouring onto the floor. The beakers are put away. He sucks the water from his hands, and then begins to climb into the water-tray. He is stopped, and screams, insisting on climbing in. He is lifted down, and goes to the bathroom. He is brought back to the water-tray. He makes for the bathroom again. 'Sorry, Max, but you can't play with the taps today!' As soon as no one is looking, he sneaks into the bathroom to turn on the taps full-blast filling the sink to the brim, letting it overflow and sticking his finger up the tap, squirting water everywhere.

The almost violent degree of compulsiveness that characterises these behaviours, that leaves no awareness, quickly pervades all around. The unexpected suddenness takes everyone by surprise, leaving no time for thought or preventative adult intervention, which makes them so especially resistant to change and behaviour modification. While the child is hell-bent to climb, squirt, pour, throw, swallow, run, scavenge, always faster than lightning, the adult is often seized by a similarly hell-bent determination to prevent this. Fierce battles ensue, which the child usually wins with ease (see Jazzy, p. 57) – though not in his own best developmental interests. The autistic child's mind is caught in a vicious circle, whose centrifugal force spins all his own mental capacities out of existence, like some invisible hurricane. Even adults who are usually able to respond sensitively and thoughtfully find themselves swept away by this bewildering cyclonic force that makes thinking very difficult – with devastating results: nobody understands, nobody knows what to do.

It is here that the autistic child parts company with us, trapped in his anti-developmental vicious circle. Whatever big or minor problem there may be that would need some tolerance and thinking to find a suitable solution, he gets rid of 'it' because he cannot think about 'it'; and he cannot think about 'it', because he has not developed the mental structures and processes that are necessary for thinking, because he has always got rid of 'it' before these could develop. Because he has never developed his thinking skills, he has nothing to think with and nothing to think about. He cannot get a grip on his mind, to enable him to use his mental and cognitive skills competently and effectively. In order not to be overwhelmed by an unmanageable situation, he finds himself compelled to get rid of whatever problem comes his way in a less mental, a more direct and concrete way: 'out of sight – out of mind' in the truest sense of the word. Before he could have made use of whatever could have helped him develop his cognitive skills and thinking capacities, whatever had triggered the need for this, it is gone: thrown, swallowed, bitten off, knocked off, tipped out, screamed to death, left behind. This is perhaps one of the biggest stumbling-blocks to the autistic child's cognitive development, and learning in general.

To the autistic child, life and events have not become meaningful in the same way we take so absolutely for granted. His world does not make sense. His mind is ill-equipped to deal with the emotional content it relates to. His feelings are not meaningful to him, nor is what other people do, think and feel. His world is dominated by appearances, which he clings to like a ship-wrecked sailor to a wooden plank. If he feels thrown up and down by inner waves of unnameable feelings, he clings even more ferociously to his plank. If dark shapes appear somewhere in the distance (or paint or glue on the table, or bits on the floor) or something feels sharp to the touch of his hands or eye (like sharp-looking legs sticking out of play-animals), he bites and swallows what might attack him, he screams to scare off any frightening persecutor (including his mother and key-worker when they want to play with him); he struggles to get away, he fights, runs or climbs for his life. He does not, he cannot stop, think about it, find other ways of dealing with it. He does not realise he could hitch a ride on the fishing boat, or the dolphin that keeps playing around him – or sit down and play with that adult who has been trying to make contact with him, unsuccessfully, all this time.

Our aim must be to get across to him that 'it' is in fact not quite so bad, so dangerous, so awful. We want to find ways to show him that there are some fun things we can do with those dark scary shapes and feelings – if we do them *together*. This will be easier with some autistic children than with others. While Patrick accepted such offers eagerly, a child like Max needed much more perseverance from the adult to dare give it a try. With children like Kofi and Tim it often seemed impossible, because they seemed so uninterested, almost as if determined to keep out any interference with their status quo. But – who can say whether with patience, sensitivity and perseverance even a child like Kofi might suddenly glimpse a bit of fun in playing with us, rather than running away from undefinable 'its'?

A little later Max is taken to another room where paint and glue have been put out. He grabs a glue-pot and, quick as lightning, sucks glue from his fingers before anyone can stop him. Reluctantly he agrees to sit down. While being given a spreader he has already grabbed another glue-pot to eat more glue. When I take it, to put the spreader into his hand instead, he screams, kicks back the chair and reaches for another child's glue-pot. The child screams in protest, Max grabs harder and screams too ... Taken away from the glueing activity, he runs away and pushes a child off the chair she is sitting on, to climb onto the drawing-table again. She resists and screams, Max pulls her harder, and I intervene: 'Sorry, Max. But there's *no climbing!*' A teacher comes to comfort the little girl. Max drifts over to the sand-tray. Before I can get there (and I am pretty fast!), he has thrown two handfuls of sand over other children. The children scream, a new mother rushes to brush sand off her little boy, his key-worker apologises. I hand Max a bucket and spade, keeping my eyes on his hands and my hands within an inch of his. He screams when I stop him from throwing more sand and chucks bucket and spade instead. 'It's a good opportunity to practise my patience', I think to myself, feeling exasperated, helpless and not far from wanting to shake him or run away myself. Then I think of Max and what he may be feeling: the same exasperated frustration, maybe? 'Gosh, it's frustrating! What *can* Max do?' I offer in an attempt to catch and contain both our exasperated feelings in words. I feel I have been chasing after him for hours – but when I check the time, only an eternal-seeming twenty-five minutes have passed!

Deciding that both of us need cheering up I throw him in the air and catch him. He laughs. 'Oh, good', I think, 'now we've got a game!' and I put him down. He wants me to do it again. I wait for him to 'ask'. I am prepared to wait for a long time, but also to accept any genuine communicative attempt from him. He tugs on my clothes. 'Oh, you want something from me?' – I pretend to be a quite a bit slower in understanding than I really am: 'What exactly do you want me to do?' Speaking in a dramatic and larger-than-life manner I manage to attract him to look at my face and I make all the effort I can to hold his attention firmly with my eyes and responsively smiling face. I take his hands and ask him 'What is it you want?' and 'What can Max do?', while playfully pulling him to and fro in a rhythm, in what the famous child-development expert Gesell calls 'gross-motor humour' (1943). Max laughs and looks at my face. This is the cue I had been waiting for, and I throw him up again. ... For the first time today, it feels good being together. We play like this for a little while. Then he wanders off, towards the bathroom. I say a playfully threatening 'I am watching you!?!' He turns to give me the briefest of grins – and walks to the easel instead! I am stunned.

The day continues much as above, but with one big difference: Max and I now have a shared understanding of a mutual game, that even Max finds more fun than his lonely climbing, throwing or water-play. While at first he had appeared so lost, wandering around, throwing something here, climbing somewhere there, in a world without meaning, with nothing in it he really seemed to enjoy, now something does make human sense. Where, before, nothing seemed to make sense, where he seemed driven just to get away from whatever was on offer by climbing, not settling and walking away, where he was driven to get rid of whatever could have occupied him by swallowing or throwing, where nothing seemed to be worth paying attention to or playing with – there is now our shared game of 'gross-motor humour', that makes sense just because both of us know and understand our game: he knows that I know that he knows what our shared game is. I know what is likely to catch his attention and make a big effort to hold it, and he gradually realises that I think that he can play a more actively communicative part in our game, than he had come to think. Suddenly, during those little interactive moments, 'getting rid' of 'it' is no longer the most pressing thing for Max. Suddenly it is more important to keep this game going, to get me to do whatever just made him laugh. This means he is motivated to communicate with another person. What a change from the boy before, who was so intent only on getting away and getting rid of whatever 'it' was!

With his little backward glance, that so clearly was a communication addressed to me, Max had also shown how much he needs someone to keep him in mind, to keep their eyes on him and to remind him that he is not alone. It also indicated how much Max is aware of, and appreciates it, when someone keeps him 'live company'. But before I could do so, I had to stand in his way in order to make enough of an impact for Max to take note of me. Had I not done so, I would just have become another 'it' to be brushed away and got rid of. Only once he had come up against the wall which was me, blocking him again and again from climbing, throwing, eating glue, flooding the floor, and other essentially mindless 'get rid of' activities, was he able to notice that I was there, and had some unsuspected human uses. But I had not just confronted him with a brick wall. I had shown him that, while there were firm and solid boundaries, for example 'no climbing', 'no throwing', 'no flooding', he was safely held and contained by the firm focus of my mind on him, not unlike an unborn baby by its mother's womb (see chapter 7). Every time he came up against me or happened to look into my eyes, he found me totally focussed on him. This helped Max in turn to focus and to manage to pull himself together, as is apparent from his little backward glance. It felt as if he in fact wanted me to stop him from mindlessly trying to get rid of everything, and to show him something else to do. It is important not to leave such a young child alone with our boundary and the 'no!', but to facilitate the transition for him. In this way, Max may learn a little of what it takes to deal with the unfamiliar, rather than just getting rid of 'it'. Needless to say, I was exhausted. But had it not been worth it?!

Like a Net with a Hole in It: On Knots, Nets and Metaphors

Having our efforts to engage the autistic child ignored is hard to tolerate, leaving us riddled with painful emotions – feeling helpless, incompetent and out of our depth. So often our communications seem to disappear in some invisible hole. Experience teaches us that we have to make 'it' bigger (whatever 'it' is) and when we do, it is usually possible to catch and hold his attention. His mind and mental functioning sometimes seem like a net with an additional big hole somewhere so that even larger items fall through. Whether biologically correct or not, the image of 'a net with a hole in it' is a metaphor with substantial power to guide us in our search for appropriate ways of reaching him.

Without having to be a brain specialist thinking of brain-cell connections, we can play with the idea that if something we say, something the child sees or hears, happens to hit a 'knot' then he may respond. But if it hits in between our imaginary 'knots', then he does not receive the information he needs to respond. This means that sometimes he may hear what we say, sometimes not, like the hit and miss in a game of 'Battleships'. Perhaps he only has very few 'ships' on his game sheet, making it very hard for us to score a hit. If we try out different ways, use different words, say it in different tones of voice, including varying our movements and gestures, waiting patiently and expectantly for delayed reactions, then our chances of hitting a 'knot' increase.

Adrian seemed to hear whatever was said to him like some kind of wind: nothing there – just a breeze around his ears, a wind (sometimes a storm) of sounds. But he did respond to the emotional ebb and flow of the music of someone speaking to him, to 'I'm gonna getcha' games of all kinds – although with a delay much longer than most adults remembered to wait and watch for.

The autistic child may listen to voices and sounds like a 'sound blanket' that wraps around him in a comforting way, or like a plaster to patch up that hole in the net. He has no idea that these sounds and voices may carry meaning, expecting some kind of action from him. He may be letting the sounds of loud or gentle words waft past him, no more than some kind of background noise which he ignores, just as we ignore the constant hum of the fridge or the racket of the power drill from the building site outside. For Adrian to respond, there had to be a huge element of suspense and excitement in the adult's voice, and even then his response was delayed, as if his mental processing was ticking more slowly, or the holes in his 'net' were bigger than we were prepared for. Derek's mind also seemed to need more time to find a responsive 'knot':

Derek often looked away and seemed to listen as if to far-away sounds or something inside him. If his worker wanted him to come, she had to call several times. At first she thought he was ignoring her or did not hear. But then she stopped to watch what would happen when she kept her attention focussed on him. She found to her surprise, that although he ran away as if she had said nothing, he would come drifting past her shortly after. Until I pointed it out, it had not occurred to her that perhaps this was Derek's way of responding. She realised that he would come – though with such delay that by that time she had usually given up hope, until she learnt to wait for much longer.

Both children could respond to the adult's calls and enjoyed the human company offered. But they needed much more time together with carefully tailored, lively human encouragement, the result of patient observations. The autistic child needs to be held together by the adult's attentive and observant mind, which serves to gather the net, catching his attention like a shoal of glittering fish and hauling it in. With such support they were able to draw their senses into a communicative appetite for spontaneous interaction they both enjoyed.

The autistic child finds it so difficult to pull his senses together. His mind may have drifted off, and he may not know how to retrieve it from where it has gone. He may have become lulled into some dream-like state that cancels out all his mental capacities of awareness, so he does indeed not hear, see or notice what is going on around him. He may be reluctant to return to the outside world, and because this state of cut-off-ness which he has drifted into, is such a soft, warm and pleasant one, he does not want to leave without very good reason. When Anne Alvarez' little autistic patient Robby eventually began to be able to put his experiences into words, he talked about 'a long, long stocking' that was needed to reach him in the far-away states of mind where he had spent most of his life. He said he felt so far away, as if he had fallen into a deep, deep hole that it needed something very, very long (i.e. a person who was very very patient, alert, firm and determined) to reach him (Alvarez 1992). The autistic child's mental state may be such that he needs us to continually throw him a lifeline, so he can pull himself out of the persistent mind-holes he keeps falling into.

Another useful net metaphor is the old-fashioned shopping-net, which is good for carrying large items. But anything small will fall through the holes (except when in a paper bag). Such a net is only functional when carried by someone. As soon as it is put down the whole caboodle falls apart, with bits spilling everywhere: a wonderfully helpful image to guide our thinking about the autistic child, whose mind sometimes seems like a net with bits of 'shopping' in it, i.e. perceptions and experiences (Spensley 1985). In order to be functional, someone has to be holding it together for him (some insist on being carried all the time). But it is not physical holding he needs so urgently. It is being picked up and held together *mentally* by an adult's focussed mind.

Without such images or metaphors for guidance it is easy to get very lost about how to treat the autistic child who is ignoring us. Getting increasingly frustrated, an angry, exasperated element can easily sneak into one's sense of helplessness. Feeling provoked by his unresponsiveness, people may find themselves wanting to correct such unacceptable behaviour, to 'drive it out of him' by force:

> Harvey was lying on his tummy on the floor rubbing himself while watching TV. His father said 'Sit up, Harvey.' No response. He called again, louder – then sharply 'Harvey! Sit up!' Again no response. Dad reached for a stick and tapped it on the settee. Harvey gave a frightened glance and sat up on his knees. Later, his hand inside his trousers, his dad called 'Hand out, Harvey' and tapped his stick again. Harvey whimpered and pulled out his hand. Later again, Dad called Harvey to give him a kiss. Mum laughed when Harvey obeyed, reluctantly, keeping as much distance as possible to get away again quickly.

Harvey's dad was a kind man and he says that he never used his stick to hit Harvey. But Harvey seemed to respond because he was scared of the stick, not because he was responding to his dad. It did not help Harvey develop the fleeting interest he had in other people. Instead it further linked social contact with being frightened, which is counterproductive. His dad used a threat, and it seemed to work. But did it really? And at what cost? Applying the image of the net, it seems like a really big knot made from existing threads. But it is a knot of fear, creating even bigger holes all around. A threatening stick, being harshly pulled by the arm, a shrill voice full of angry irritation, may bring the autistic child back with a jerk. But it is also likely to increase his desire to return as quickly as possible to his dreamy state of non-involvement, of letting the world drift by, and to extend his time there as much as he can. Harvey's father may have helped his son to tie a knot – but there are anti-developmental knots as well as growth-promoting. Fear does not promote healthy development of a person's mind. It does not promote friendly relationships, which we so desperately want to foster.

If our aim is to awaken his interest in other people and human communication, then we must make the enormous effort to summon up huge amounts of patience, to wait for longer, to give the autistic child much more time to respond than we may think. Coming from a position of understanding his plight, we will call – and call again, a little bit different every time, combining understanding with firmness, trying to knit a better net for and with him. Do we simply want him to obey, 'blindly', to our commands, or do we want to discover ways that allow him to respond *because he wants to?*

Harvey was one of those highly sensitive and anxious autistic children, but with quite a bit of interest in people and social communication to tap into. He liked looking into other people's faces, but he seemed to forget about it. When reminded by someone's face appearing in his line of vision, or when he found his movements echoed, he would respond with a surprised and delighted look.

I knew that Harvey's parents were aware of their son's non-autistic potential and keen to help him develop this in any way they could, and we met to discuss my concerns. Mum knew immediately what I meant, and Dad explained that he just did not know what else to do. But he was convinced that Harvey switched off his mind at times, whether deliberately or because he could not help it. Dad had a healthy common-sense attitude, and was clearly trying to help his son to tighten his 'net' to create more 'knots' of healthy human connection. He had not thought of using his voice and face, instead of his stick, to attract and hold Harvey's attention. He tried it, and it worked. Not only that, it gave him a lot more smiles from Harvey, and greatly reduced the tension that had been building up at home.

We need to be clear about our aims. Do we want to train him to conform and obey, or do we want to nurture and encourage his interest in other people and social activities? Do we believe that there is some communicative social potential in every human being including the autistic child? Or do we believe that the autistic child is fundamentally different from other children and from ourselves, that he has no need for human company, for social communication and interactive fun? Do we believe that an autistic child is autistic through and through? Or are there non-autistic parts and aspects which are like any other child, with healthy communicative 'knots' that can connect responsively with another person? Even if he seems not to think so, can we, and do we want to, imagine that it may be possible to claim or reclaim him into human company, and to help him to 'tighten the net'?

We don't make a weak plant or a puppy grow by shouting at it or hitting it with a stick. Hitting the net with a stick will stop neither cherries nor potatoes falling out. We cannot force a flower-bud to open before its time by pulling down its petals. Such treatment will only result in damage to the developing flower. We need to water and feed the plant, place it in the right kind of light. After that we have to stand back to watch carefully for signs of limp or shiny leaves, stunted or healthy growth, dropped or swelling flower-buds: the plant's communications that things are well, or not. If we want to save an ailing plant, we need carefully to try out which little changes are needed to remedy the situation. Does it need more water, or less, more light or less? Is there a draught, is the pot too small? In the same way we must observe the autistic child carefully to find out how we can encourage his communicative and social potential to grow.

Something that does not usually occur to people, but that works almost every time, is to make use of the playful surprise element of paradoxical responses. The surprise of the unexpected often acts like a drawstring, pulling together the loose net of the autistic child's mind into one focus. Even the single cherry will stay in the net when taken by surprise by our hand, unexpectedly covering the hole it was just about to fall out of. This is only possible with the adult's very focussed attention to detailed movement, be that in the child, or the cherry. With careful self-observation, we will discover that our repertoire of responses is much greater than we thought.

Try, for example, to whisper instead of getting louder, to speak more slowly or softly when your irritation wants to make you speak harsher, faster, louder. Take a step back instead of towards him, withdraw your hand when you were about to grab his arm, stand up suddenly, just when he thought you were going to sit down, or turn away when he thought you were coming to get him.

If done in a deliberate and disciplined way, with your mind focussed closely on the child, he will feel a sense of surprise, with a general tightening surging through the net. He had hardened against a sense that something was coming at him. He had withdrawn from all such 'unpleasantries'. But suddenly this is not happening. 'What is going on? Something was getting at me just now. Where is it gone?' It tugs at his innate curiosity. It pulls the net of his attention tight. He wants to catch it. Even if it does not make him look up, it lessens his defences. If you watch very closely, you may see a subtle softening in his bodily tension, a slight movement of his head indicating a focussing of his attention, an opening of his ears to a more interested receptiveness. His eyes have certainly noticed and followed your controlled retreat, even if he did not seem to be looking (don't forget that peripheral vision is a powerful secret scanning and surveillance method). Savour his surprise. You have now started a sub-version of an 'I'm gonna getcha' game (see chapter 4). Enjoy it. The issue now is no longer 'I want you to sit up' or 'Take your hand out of your trousers.' The name of the game now is a playfully teasing, interactive fun-loving 'I'm gonna getcha' game that may go on for some time, with the rather boring 'sitting up' as a possible secondary side-product a little later on. In many ways it is similar to a one- or two-year-old, who also often will not cooperate just like that, but who has to be enticed into cooperating with playful teasing or chasing games, or 'gross-motor humour' (Gesell 1943).

By aiming at the earlier developmental levels which the autistic child has (for whatever reason) missed out on, by making our facial expressions and movements more dramatic and larger-than-life, we may perhaps be able to gradually tighten the net of his social interest and to increase the knots of his attention. It is as if we had picked up the shopping-net, infused with our understanding, so it tightens and becomes functionally useful. We have also potted, fed and watered the plant, placed it outside where the sun will give it the light it needs, and the wind will challenge its stem to produce stronger roots. Other such picture analogies may come to your mind to help you with catching and holding the autistic child's attention.

PART II

LET'S PLAY! – GAMES AND ACTIVITIES: PROMOTING GROWTH AND DEVELOPMENT

4
Communication Games

Walking the Tightrope Between Fear and Delight: 'I'm Gonna Getcha' – and Other Attention-Getting Games

There is a simple game, familiar to us all, that is ideally suited to drawing the autistic child into interaction with another person. It needs no toys, no other objects, no words – just our voice. It is purely social, yet manages to demand the attention of even the most withdrawn child. The most basic of social games, sensitive adults play it spontaneously with babies as young as two months. It helps to lay the foundations for later language development. It also helps us in our search for ways to make contact with a child who is so rejecting of all our attempts to reach, play and have fun with him. It is the familiar 'I'm coming to get you!' game we all know. All children like playful chasing games: squealing with delight, the child runs away from a smiling adult who pursues him with a playful 'I'm coming to get you!' Already babies love the early version of this game, in which the adult might wiggle her finger, or slowly move her face towards the baby's tummy with a drawn-out and perhaps mysterious-sounding 'I'm gonna – [pause] – tickle your – [pause] – tummy', or 'I'm gonna –[pause] – bite your – [pause] – nose off.'

Adults who are attuned to a baby naturally develop short routines and games to enjoy together. When she is sure that the child likes the game, or to check whether he remembers, the adult begins to build up an atmosphere of suspense and anticipation, slowly moving towards him – but then she pauses, waiting for him to look, make a sound or movement, to indicate that he is expecting the tickle, or whatever it is. If he shows no sign of anticipation, the adult generally takes a big dramatic gasp to alert his curiosity and expectancy. Expressive of a feeling of alarm, this provokes eye contact and an orienting response that is innate, dating back to our animal ancestors. Babies quickly learn the basic format of this game, which consists almost exclusively of the fact that it always ends with some kind of pleasurable physical contact. The child comes to know the routine, to expect the tickle, the cuddle, to be picked up or swung around. The rules of the game are so simple, so predictable, that it could easily be boring. But it is perhaps one of the most exciting basic games.

What makes it exciting is that the timing is totally unpredictable. Because the adult playfully extends suspense and mock threat, constantly moving forward or retreating, the child can never let his attention sag. He can hardly wait for the delicious tickle, yet he never knows exactly when it is coming: 'is it now or not yet – or now or ... or ... or when?' This introduces an element of uncertainty and suspense, a need to be alert and vigilant. Having to keep his mind focussed on the supposed 'threat' is like *walking a mental–emotional tightrope between fear and delight*: waiting to see whether we really are, or aren't, going to do 'it', and what this 'it' is, commands all his attention. He feels compelled to check our face for clues of our intentions, which means genuine communicative eye contact.

This game provides, for the autistic child and the baby alike, a clear structure, or 'scaffolding', to slot in whatever skills he has for social interaction. It seems to be made up not so much of the behaviours of two individuals, as of a dynamic and constantly changing web of interpersonal events always responding to each other. It also taps into the child's deepest layers of emotional experience, his dreading, and at the same time wanting, 'to be got', to be tickled. The 'pretend-threat' attracts his attention on a physical survival or gut level, engaging his attention, motivation and interest – fundamental for cognitive and mental functioning to develop.

Adrian spent most of his time trundling from one end of the room to the other, taking no notice of anything around him. But when I crept after him, making him aware of my pursuit by saying 'I'm – [pause] – gonna – [pause] – getcha!', putting as much excitement-demanding and playful pretend-threatening suspense into my tone of voice as I possibly could, then he would turn around to assess the extent of my 'threat'. Should he run for cover? Or try to dodge whatever was coming to get him? Which way was it coming, and which way should he turn?

But on turning round he made two unexpected discoveries: instead of the expected threat, he found himself surprised by a broad, encouraging, playful smile on my face and wide beaming eyes. To add to his surprise I would also suddenly stop dead, or even take a step back, thus further contradicting my earlier suggestion of being a threat and coming to get him. *The adult's constant readiness to stop or retreat is crucial, in order to make the game unmistakably playful and non-threatening.*

The moment I could see that he had assessed the situation and taken in the fact that I wanted to play with him, and was not actually threatening him, I would begin slowly, and with as much mysterious drama in my movements as possible, to creep up on him again. For some moments both of us would now be looking each other in the eye, firmly focussed on each other, and what the other was going to do next. Attentions were taut like an arrow about to be shot. This kind of awareness and social interest in an interaction with another person was a great achievement for Adrian.

Next he would run off, giggling and chuckling, with backward glances to check how close I had come and to prepare his escape if necessary, thoroughly enjoying our little chasing game. Again I would make an approach, just slightly different each time – this time perhaps touching him. But contrary to his expectations, I would immediately and surprisingly step back again, smiling perhaps mischievously. I might add a further excitement-generating drawn-out 'I'm gonna getcha -', but then retreat all of a sudden, unexpectedly changing my mind again to 'Oh no, I'm not.'

With Adrian this was particularly important, as he (unlike other children) did not like to be caught. Too much physical contact scared him, and I made sure never to overstep this mark, never to betray his trust in me. We now had not only a shared topic or game, but also a shared understanding of each other, so crucial for the development of social interest. It even included the more subtle understanding of knowing what the other person knows: Adrian knew that I knew that he didn't like me to actually get him, and that he could trust me not to, but that he enjoyed the game as long as it was played according to these rules.

With interaction so firmly scaffolded, and the constant pretend-danger of falling off that precarious imaginary tightrope helping to focus their mind, many autistic children surprise themselves, and us, to find the resources within themselves to respond. The anticipation of the supposed pretend-threat counteracts his tendency to let his senses, and with that his mind or cognitive functioning, fall apart into purely sensory experience, devoid of meaning. The anticipation of the unpredictably timed thrill acts like a magnet, drawing together the elements of his mind like iron filings, connecting his senses of listening and hearing, looking and seeing, which makes expectation, thinking, appropriate responsiveness and cognitive functioning possible.

With the less active, more withdrawn autistic child, who may spend much of his time somewhere doing nothing in particular, the 'I'm gonna ... !'

game needs to be like the early version we play with the ordinary baby long before he is mobile and moving around.

It sometimes seemed as if the developmentally earlier sitting down version of the game was the only game Tim enjoyed. Lying on a bean-bag I sat near him to try to attract his attention. I talked to him a little about what was going on, what he might be thinking or feeling. He would turn his head away, brushing my face with the briefest glance, indicating that he was indeed aware of my presence – and perhaps vaguely interested. But he did like tickles.

I therefore took my finger through his field of vision in '*wiggly worm*' fashion, i.e. bending and stretching it in a playfully 'wiggly' rhythm, saying an extremely dramatic drawn-out 'I'm gonna tickle yooour ... tummy.' First I tried to lessen his need for avoidance and to get across to him that I was proposing something friendly and fun: you can't possibly be frightened of a silly 'wiggly worm' finger. I then built up a huge sense of anticipation and expectancy with my movements (for example making a large sweep with my finger) and tone of voice, using long drawn-out pauses to stretch the atmosphere of suspense almost to breaking-point, with the idea of summoning and holding his attention and any traces of ability and willingness to respond he might possibly be able to muster.

In this way Tim had to use a number of important mental functions, for example listening and watching, expecting my next move, wondering where it had gone, looking for it in my face, realising that my focussed attention was still firmly on him. When he responded with a smile or giggle to invite the tickle, he had taken the initiative in the game, the part of an active and communicative participator. Unwittingly, he had at the same time stretched his frustration tolerance and slightly increased his sense of social playfulness.

While some young autistic children take to this game with such pleasure, ease and delight, as if they had been waiting for someone to 'get' them all their life, with children like Tim it demands a massive amount of effort, concentration, patience and perseverance from the adult. But it *was* possible to 'get' him. And the longer I could help him stretch and hold his attention, the more practice he got in doing it – and in feeling that social interactive games with another person could be fun and worth engaging in.

Once a child knows the 'I'm gonna ... !' version of the game well, he will participate by making sounds or giving other signs of anticipation to get us to do our next move. We then want to help him move on to more mental and cognitively challenging ways, by slowly decreasing the emphasis on the sensuous tickle. While all the build-up of suspense and expectancy remains the same, we may change the tickle to a mere touching, perhaps combined with learning the names of the body parts: 'I'm gonna – touch yoooouuur ... nose/ arm/ feet.' Next, our anticipatory pause may *follow*, rather than precede, our last word 'I'm gonna touch yoooouuur nose/ arm/ feet .... !', waiting for him to respond first, by focussing his attention on the named body part, perhaps withdrawing or protecting the 'threatened' part, for example by covering his nose, withdrawing his arm, moving his feet. Here too we may suddenly change our mind and stop dead in full flow with 'Oh no, I'm not. I think I'll touch your ears/ clap my hands instead.'

If the child is a listener, we could crunch up some tissue-paper or ring some bells to encourage him to look and focus his attention. Such a sound game can easily be made into an 'I'm gonna ... beat the drum' or 'Oh, no, I've changed my mind and I will simply hold it still, here within your reach.' If said and acted in an exaggerated excitement-generating way, then he may even reach out and beat the drum himself. With all these games, the adult aim is to create an atmosphere of great suspense and excitement, of 'walking a tightrope between fear and delight'.

'There and Gone!' Playing with Distance: Running Away = Inviting You to Play?

'Playing with distance' is an important tool in our attempts to generate the young autistic child's interest in communication and interaction, which means that we must train our own awareness of the child's and our own use of distance. We all have our field of personal space which must not be transgressed in order not to feel invaded: someone just standing a few inches too close makes us back off automatically with a sense of apprehension. The speed with which someone approaches us, for example briskly walking up very close to us, also makes us tense up.

Many autistic children are hypersensitive concerning their own personal space, the right kind of distance, and the *movement* of decreasing or increasing distance. Some simply get up and walk away as soon as someone comes towards them. The adult's response to the child's running away is usually to turn away and walk off herself, feeling disappointed, rejected and helpless. She may think 'Gosh, this is hopeless. There's nothing I can do.' This is where our conscious awareness of our thoughts, feelings and actions is at its most crucial:

Kofi's key-worker desperately wanted to engage him. As soon as he sat somewhere by himself, she sat close, putting a cause-and-effect toy on his lap or bouncing a ball to him, sometimes in silence, sometimes talking loudly about what he should do. It never worked. Why did he get up and walk away every time? In her opinion it showed how very autistic he was.

Another worker would begin by calling his name in an exciting-sounding voice while walking up to him. Before sitting down she took a big 'mock-shocked' in-breath saying a dramatic 'Oh, *look!* [pausing for suspense] Look, what *I've* got!', even if it was nothing more than the ball they played with yesterday. With that he'd look up with a mixture of surprise and apprehension, giving her the clue she needed to feel that she could sit down near him. But doing so she detected a tiny movement indicating that Kofi was about to get up (and presumably run off). Immediately the worker moved to sit just a fraction further away than she had intended – and Kofi stayed. For a few moments, she waited silently and very still, just holding the ball poised in mid-air where he could see and reach it, but not too near. Her sudden and unexpected stillness – after she had so clearly come to do something with him, surprised him again. He looked into her face to see what she was up to now. She smiled and greeted him with a gentle 'Hello!?', then rolled the ball to him. He grabbed it – and their game had begun.

As it is a natural impulse to move closer and *towards* somebody to get their attention, we have to make a conscious effort to include movements *away* from him into our game. The child is teetering between being interested and feeling overwhelmed, persecuted and threatened, about to run or cut off. If we notice this just before it happens, just before he 'goes over the brink', then we can retreat, for example move our head back, step back physically (thus increasing the distance), lower our voice, slow down our speaking or our movements. We can even stop dead completely, in an expectant, rather than a hopeless way, like a poised bow held taut and ready, in an attitude of utmost suspense, to go off at just the right moment – all the time closely watching his reaction. Perhaps it is an old animal instinct: when something apparently alive which we felt threatened by in some way recedes, we are compelled to check where it has gone, where it is going and whether or not it is still out to get us. He will look into our face with puzzled curiosity – at which moment there is not only eye contact, but a moment of real human communication, joy and interaction, a moment of the crucial 'shared attention'. If this is a natural instinct that helps the autistic child unlock his human and interactive potential, then let's make the most of it.

We need to notice how, and how much, we have moved our body and our head, to pay close attention to how close we are sitting, to the manner and speed with which we sat down, the expression on our face and how we are using our voice at each moment, what we are saying, how loud, how fast, how softly, or whether we did not speak or made no sound at all. Did we, perhaps, sit down in that imposing way that has a demanding 'You *will* do this with me now!' feel to it? Or did it have a much softer 'Hello, wouldn't it be nice to play together?' quality, that is so much more child-centred? Did we approach him in a sudden way, pushing a toy under his nose rather harshly and forcefully (perhaps already steeling ourselves to the expected rejection), or were we announcing our imminent appearance by gently talking about what we were about to do, slowly coming closer and perhaps tapping the toy? Were we using our movements and the music in our voice to stir his curiosity and create an atmosphere of excitement and suspense?

It is surprising how much difference subtle changes in our posture, approach, speed and distance can make in facilitating communication with a young autistic child. Some children will stay if you make a tiny movement *away*, that is, to sit about two inches further from them, the very moment they make as if to get up and run away. It is helpful to add quietly in simple words what just happened: '"Oops, not too close", says Kofi', or if you did not move away quickly enough or he took flight: 'Oops, too close. Adrian didn't like that.'

Adrian seemed to fly away like a bird as soon as anyone moved towards him. After much patient trial and error I discovered that I could engage him if, instead of moving towards him, I did just the opposite, i.e. step or move my head back. Then he would turn around every time while running away, as if thinking 'Oops, where is it gone? – I thought it was coming to get me.' I could then show him with my smiling face and softly speaking voice, that I was *not* coming to get him in a scary way, but that I had also not gone away or given up. On the contrary, I still wanted us to play.

The child who is about to run away, to cut off and withdraw, will be almost unable to do so, if the source of what made him feel threatened is unexpectedly gone. He will have to stay to check where it has disappeared to: somehow it seems to have stopped coming from nearby, or the left, or wherever. His mental capacities are thus pulled together and focussed on locating the disruption of his expectation. As the disruption is caused by you, he will find the smiling face of a friendly human being at the other end of his search. He is puzzled: 'This is strange. ... So there wasn't a scary thing threatening me? ... She's smiling. This is actually quite nice. ... I wonder what she is going to do next. ...' These thoughts (although perhaps only there as some sense of curiosity) are a truly social communicative link.

With the more passive autistic child, how close you sit is not so important, as he avoids you anyway by turning his head away, averting or closing his eyes, and shutting off his mind. But if you paradoxically *increase* the distance by moving away a little, after a few gentle rounds of 'I'm gonna getcha!', while also talking to him quietly to alert him to your friendly presence, you can attract his attention. Provided you move your head and body a little within his field of vision, he will be unable to avoid noticing you, even if he keeps his eyes mostly averted, as movement attracts visual attention:

> The only way to get Tim's attention, when he was staring into the 'non-seeing distance' was the *'away*-movement': approached with a 'wiggly worm finger' or an 'I'm gonna getcha!' game, he simply turned his head or shut his eyes. But if the 'wiggly worm finger' that had been coming at him, suddenly *retreated* or *disappeared*, he turned every time to look with disconcerted surprise wondering 'Where has it gone?'

Another useful interpretation is to regard the child's walking away as a positive response, rather than as a rejection. OK, he walked away. But he also responded. A response is a communication – in this case, a communication from a non-communicating child.

> We can join him in *his* version of the game when he runs off by saying: 'Yes, you are right: I came. And you said "byebye"', followed by 'I can still see you: hello Adrian!', just as we would do spontaneously with any one-year-old. When he passes by you again some moments later, you can greet him with a delighted 'Hello. There you are. You came back', before he leaves you again to run off and repeat the new 'there and gone' game he himself has just introduced you to.

From this perspective, the child's running away turns from being a rejection to being an invitation to a 'come and get me' or a 'can you still see me?' game, which is interactive. We have achieved our original goal of trying to engage him in playful interaction, except with a delay of several minutes, and with the game not initiated by you but by an autistic child. Fortunately, we are not as impatient and bossy as a young child (at least I hope not) and have learnt to wait. Of course we prefer the initiative to come from the child himself. If seen in this way, the adult need not feel so rejected and useless, and the child not such a hopeless case. Instead both of you can take away a sense of joy, of play, of being successful.

> Fatima spent most of the time running to and fro, climbing on window-sills and furniture. She never sat down to play, and it seemed impossible to engage her in any interaction or game. But one day when she was in the play house on her own, I looked in through the door. She gave me the greatest of smiles, and I came in, taking her smile as invitation. But she walked straight past me and out of the house, leaving me to feel stupid: had I misunderstood her, made her feel pushed out? Making a

mental note of my thoughts and feelings, I stayed where I had been left and turned to see what she was up to.

To my great surprise, she was standing by the book rack, searchingly looking up and down. She finally chose a photo book, 'First Words', the only book she had ever been interested in, and took it to the big chair. Curious as to what her plans were, I had been watching her quietly, delighted (in fact, holding my breath) that she so clearly seemed to *have* a plan. Climbing on the chair, she opened the book and turned the pages as if looking for a particular picture. Having now joined her I said 'I wonder which page you are looking for ... Is it the food-page?'(her favourite). It was. She 'tickled' the raisins as if wanting to pick them up, then looked around the page. I named and pointed to what I thought she was looking at or interested in, before she got up to look for another book.

Although it seems that I had been wrong to interpret Fatima's smile as an invitation for me to come closer, and that it may have been better had I stayed where I was, joining her from the outside, the events that followed suggest that she had, nevertheless, taken on board my offer to be with her in a big way. But she was unable to ask for my attention or to show that she wanted it in any more direct way. As long as I was at a distance, she could see me and did not feel threatened. But as soon as I came in, I turned into something less friendly and she felt that her personal space had been invaded. Our interaction was almost totally reliant on my being very observant, on not giving up when she left me behind, and on actively keeping my attention on her all the time. She was then able to do things she had never done before, like pretending to pick up raisins from a picture, or to look for another book. This observation shows how Fatima's running away was in fact her most important way of being in communication with me, an invitation to play and interact, and to be attentive. What a shame it would have been, what a sad loss of an opportunity, had I misinterpreted her running away as rejection.

'Ready – Steady – Push!':
Practising Pre-verbal Skills:
Shared Attention, Waiting and Taking Turns

Almost every activity can be made into a 'ready – steady – go' game, whether indoor or out, play or daily chores. Among the simplest of games, it practises the three most important skills necessary for language development:

1. 'shared attention' or looking together,
2. copying what you do or show him,
3. turn-taking, which includes being able to *wait* for one's turn.

The foundation of communicative and social development is the capacity for shared attention – looking at something *together*, doing an activity *together*, singing a song *together*. The child needs to be able to share something that interests him with another person without wanting to have it, to enjoy the mental activity of sharing an idea, rather than the self-absorbed sensual one of having (or eating) it. He needs to be able to draw our attention to what he is looking at, for example a bird in the sky, a bus across the road, and to follow with his eyes what we are showing him. Without being able to initiate and enjoy such shared attention, without being able and motivated to copy the sounds you make, he cannot learn the names of these things and how to say the words. Without being able to take turns, waiting for the other to finish, one cannot have a conversation.

But anything 'together' is not part of the autistic child's agenda. He wants to do everything by himself, or have us do it for him, and exactly his way. He does not know how much he is missing out this way, how much he really needs it, how much more fun he could have, were he to learn the joys of shared attention and sharing. He lacks both practice and experience.

By making an activity into a 'ready – steady – go!' game we show him a format, a routine, that is simple, predictable, repeatable and at the same time communicative and social. It is highly adaptable, allows infinite variations and never becomes boring, creating a situation of anticipation, excitement and suspense that becomes irresistible provided the adult exaggerates enough and puts enough dramatic pauses into her spoken and body language – like an archer, slowly and deliberately stretching her bow as far as it will go, and then waiting, waiting, waiting, in total suspense, body, mind and bow stretched to almost breaking point, until the right moment when it is finally, finally time to let go. This way the autistic child's attention is gathered into one point of focus. Our suspense acts as an attention-gathering force for him. At this moment adult and child are engaged in 'shared attention'.

The anticipation created by the adult's suspense has the power to make the child take his turn, in order to end the tension, for example by looking, making a sound or gesture. Doing so he shows that he has learnt the sequence of events you had shown him. Later he may also copy the ' – go!', which to him becomes a magic word that makes the tension go. Eventually many autistic children will say the entire sequence of 'ready – steady – go', which means that the 'non-communicating' child is communicating cooperatively in a situation of shared attention, the withdrawn child is involved in an interactive social turn-taking game and enjoying it, the silent child is making sounds (provided you wait long enough with your arrow poised), and the impulsive child waits for his turn or asks for it. I have yet to meet the child who does not come to love this game – provided you stretch that imaginary bow enough to build up such an enormous arch of anticipation together with the patience, and confidence, to stretch this out for as long as is humanly possible (usually about ten times longer than we at first think we, or the child, can tolerate).

The autistic child who loves swings, for example, normally lets you do all the work. He expects you to do the pushing, while he sits back letting the world swing by. But he could have even more fun with a game of 'ready – steady – go'. So we suggest teaching him. If we stand facing him on the swing, he can see our face and we can see his. After a few pushes to get into the swing of things, we give a demonstration by pulling back the swing with the child in it *as if* to push it. But instead we stop, holding it just there and saying the most exaggerated and excitement-generating 'ready – steady -!' – getting louder and bigger and more and more exciting, increasing anticipation and suspense almost to breaking point – until, all of a sudden, we let go of the swing with a dramatic '– aaaa-nd – pu-sh!'. Throughout we watch his face for signs of excitement or frustration, always ready to adapt, our eyes focussed on his with the biggest beaming smile.

We are prepared to wait for him to take his turn to let us know that he wants us to get on with it. We must be prepared to out-wait him for however long it takes. We must trust that he *does* have the ability to respond, at first accepting any sound, look, gesture or movement from him to get the swing moving again. We echo his communication, including his perhaps irritated 'eh-eh!', or rephrasing it into 'Yes, that's right: push', and we let the swing go – but only for three times. We hold it again and repeat the performance. After some time, we include a hugely stretched-out pause of suspense after the first 'ready' in anticipation of some contribution from him for the now anticipated 'steady', and again, and even more stretched out, before the 'go!' or the 'push!'

After several runs, probably over the course of some days or weeks, depending on each child, we gradually increase our expectation for him to join in and play his part in the game (= turn-taking). Provided the activity is enough fun and we stretch out our pause, like an elastic band, edging him on with our eyes and biggest smile, for as long as anyone could possibly bear it (always much longer than you think) before the desired push, he will be virtually unable to resist taking his turn by at least giving you a demanding look (= shared attention). He will probably also make some sound, initially perhaps one of irritation, spurred by his frustration over your irritating lack of automatic compliance. It is indeed a tricky juggling act, because if you wait too long for him to respond, he will explode with frustration. But if you do not wait long enough, he may continue to expect you to do all the pushing, thinking, focussing, talking, communicating – so why should he bother?

We leave gaps for him for whatever communication he wants to make. Gradually we encourage him more and more to make a sound – and finally the swing simply no longer 'works' until his vocalisation makes us let it go. With enough patience to wait long enough, perhaps prompting him with a dramatic unfinished 'pu – – ' which we leave hanging, uncomfortably, painfully, in mid-air, he will eventually be unable to stop himself from saying 'push', or at least adding the missing '–sh', to get you, for crying out loud, to let him have his swinging sensation.

Provided it does not make him fall apart completely, this game may also be played with his autistic object (see chapter 7), although usually as a much faster version at first:

> After a dramatic and excitement-generating 'ready – steady – ?' his key-worker would whizz Fred's car across the floor to him. Because she managed to make it fun enough, Fred was sure that she was not taking it away, just inserting a quick game. Eventually he whizzed it back, after she had arrived with lots of cars, rolling them to him with dramatic 'ready – steady – ... go!', encouraging, even urging him with beaming eyes, smile and excitement-generating manner to join in and return them.

Any activity can be made into such a 'ready – steady – go' game, its format providing the autistic child with a bridge to make the transitions from one activity to another, which he finds so very difficult. Putting on his shoes, taking off his jumper, washing his face, going to sit down for dinner or an activity, can all be put into exciting 'ready – steady – ... !' formats. And it does not have to end with 'go'! This will encourage him to listen and help him differentiate. Why not 'ready – steady – push' for the swing, 'ready – steady – pull' when pulling a jumper down, 'ready – steady – sit down', 'ready – steady – and shoes on', 'ready – steady – – here comes the wet flannel' or 'ready – steady – – I'll getcha!'? In this way he learns that different activities go with different words, that the same game sequence can apply to different activities, and that he can make different sounds which, in time, may even become meaningful words. Games of throwing and catching a ball, or kicking it, are also opportunities, as is jumping from a low wall, or clapping hands.

> One day in the swimming-pool I sat Jazzy next to me on the side. Our feet could reach the water. With something like alarm in my voice I started a dramatic and excitement-grabbing 'Ready! – Steady! – –Splash!!', splashing my feet in the water. 'And – – stop!', my voice building up during the 'and' before coming to an abrupt halt with 'stop'. 'And again', I said, 'ready – steady – – –'. But this time I waited for him to either say

or splash. He splashed. 'Splash!' I agreed, and we splashed. The excitement of the game was catching, and Tashan came to join us. Soon both boys added their version of 'splash': Jazzy saying 'shash' and Tashan 'psh'.

They were laughing and very excited, and I felt a bit like a lion-tamer. It required great concentration and effort to call each boy's attention all the time, and to keep them interested and joining in. After several rounds of 'ready – steady – splash', I warned them to 'Listen! –: – Ready – steady – and – *jump*!!', and I jumped into the water. So did Jazzy and Tashan. 'And up!', I announced, helping them back up onto the side. We played this for some time, with great hilarity until, all three of us sitting on the side again, feet dangling in the water, I declared 'Listen!! Ready – steady – – *splash*!!'. Both boys jumped into the water. 'No!', I said, '*Splash*, not jump!' and we repeated the sequence. We now alternated between splashing and jumping, and eventually all I had to do was to wait for one of the boys to indicate which one to do. All this lasted for a timeless eternity of about fifteen minutes, a long time for each of these autistic boys to concentrate on a task and to communicate using their voice. Fortunately it was soon time to get dressed. I was exhausted.

During this short time, both boys had grasped the rules of the 'ready – steady – go!' game, and were now keen to play it at other times and in other situations. Under the watchful guidance of an adult they were pretty good players. All these games and activities require an enormous effort from the adult, much close observation of the child's responses, and sensitive tuning-in to what he likes and is able to do. But in this way we can help a non-communicating child channel some of his abilities and activity into social communication and interaction.

The 'Away!' Game:
Playing with Rejection, Control, 'As If' and 'Pretend'

The 'Away!' game was jointly invented by three-year-old Leila and myself one day in the garden. It plays directly with the theme of rejection: who is rejecting whom, when and how, and whether the rejection is real or just 'pretend'. It allows both adult and child to take turns of being in control. It is purely interactive and relies on a combination of watching the other's subtle communicative clues and instinctive reactions, usually unaffected by the child's autism.

Leila had no speech and generally tolerated no 'interference', refusing any offers of help, screaming furiously in a way that felt solid like iron, and made people feel paralysed, even intimidated.

Up on a climbing frame, clearly wanting to climb higher, Leila kept getting stuck, screaming with outraged frustration. She seemed to 'forget' to move one hand up first (or wanted to move up without having to move it?). When I tried to help her, either by talking her through or trying to get her to shift her hand to the next bar, she screamed violently. I let go. Afraid she might lose her balance and slip, I stood close, ready to catch her. She tried to push me away. This was fantastic. Leila was choosing to interact. I put her non-verbal communication in words with an emphatic and playfully exaggerated 'Go away!' stepping back a little – only to swing right back to stand very close again.

The rhythm of all this was quite fast, its speed giving it a playfully teasing humorous feel, the quality of my movement virtually 'asking' to be pushed away again. To confirm her playful intentions I also added another exaggerated 'Away!?' with an extra dramatic pinch of invitation and humouring question in my intonation and face, which also showed a big, encouraging and interested smile.

Again Leila made a gesture as if to push me away, a big smile on her face now too, expecting me to retreat and immediately reappear again – so she could push me again. She beamed as we played, with me standing too close for a brief moment, inviting her to push me out of her personal space. Each time I added an exaggerated mock-indignant 'Away!', trying to catch in words and intonation what I thought Leila was feeling, and might have said.

Because I retreated at the slightest hint of her reaching out *as if* to push, her pushing never became more than *pretend*-pushing. This is very important: although she is not at the developmental stage of using pretend-play, the fact that already the hint of her intention to push me away was enough to send my head and body swinging back (while my eyes and attention remained firmly with her), virtually 'made' this into an early version of a pretend-game. My exaggerated responsiveness simply did not allow for a battle of wills to develop – which could easily happen if I stayed too close for just a moment too long. But I was already 'gone', before she had had the chance to really push me away.

In some ways we were playing a version of 'got you!' and 'had': the moment she reached out to push me away I was already 'gone', and the moment she thought I was 'gone' I was back, already inviting her to push me away. There was a subtle dance going on between the intentions and feelings of each of us. It had a playful and humorous quality. It was pure communication and interaction. While she was about to push and reject me, I welcomed and invited this, then returned for more – in contrast to the usual response to being pushed away, which is to feel rejected and walk away.

The next day Leila again climbed up the climbing frame. I was unsure at first about what her plans were, but as I stepped nearer, she smiled and kind of pushed me away. 'Oh, you remembered our game', I said, delighted, adding '"Away!" says Leila', and we played our new game.

When telling my collegues about our new 'Away!' game, with Leila sitting on my lap, she gently pushed my chest with her hand – letting us know how much she understands what is said. 'Away!' I picked up her offer of another round of our game, now in a new context. We had fun playing a sitting-down version, which only involved the back-and-forth movement of my upper body while saying 'away!' just before moving back the very moment she reached out with her hand. We played the 'Away!' game often, in many situations. Leila would initiate it herself; she even 'taught' it to others.

Since then I have tried this game with many other children, and found to my own surprise that most got the hang of it. Only a few, like Tim, seem so utterly immersed in their little sensory and sensuous world, that they lack the appetite for such subtle interactive games. Others manage to turn every interactive game into a sensuous experience of 'bathing in being touched' in ways that cancel out the communicative element. But many autistic children enjoy the brief contact it entails, the quick interaction and, of course, their power in being able to push away the adult effectively, again and again.

One day, a game developed between Nelson and myself: I would roll him into a 'sausage' in a gym mat, then unroll him again. When sitting on the open mat thinking what to do next, I realised he wanted me off and spotted the opportunity of a game. Getting up I said, as if speaking *for* him: 'Away!' He loved it. We played for a long time: I rolled him up, unrolled him, sat on the mat, while he pushed me 'away!', lay down for me to roll him up, ... again and again.

The more passive autistic child may not take the initiative of pushing back. But the humour and communicativeness of the moving towards him, playfully, as if to 'get him', is understood immediately by almost all children. The second part of the game, that of taking the intitiative and pushing the adult away, may need to be given time to develop.

Derek responded smilingly to the message of the little push, looking back immediately into the adult's smiling face. When called to 'come back', he came running back, laughing, and expecting to be pushed 'away!' again.

He loved this game, which meant he came to seek out interactive play. Once he knew the pattern of this game well, he also began to respond, timidly, by moving as if to push away the adult. As soon as there is a mutual understanding of the game between us and the child, we can extend the 'away!' game, eventually expecting the child to say 'away!' to continue the game.

> After some weeks, Leila began to make sounds that sounded like 'away!' She needed to be prompted very strongly, by letting tension build up before resolving a round, expectantly waiting for her to make a sound or say anything resembling 'away!' Until then I had to resolve this build-up of suspense *as if* pretending to be Leila by eventually saying 'away!' myself. But eventually she made her own sounds.

The 'away!' game allows the child to experience, play with and practise a sense of having control, of being able to protect, or defend, himself against unwanted intrusions. It gives him the sense that it is he who controls how close we are, and that he can effect change and a response – while the adult is doing the opposite of what he usually expects, i.e. moving away rather than crowding him. In some ways the adult behaves like one of those cause-and-effect toys where something happens whenever a button is pressed. But not only can we vary our response in smaller or bigger ways every time we are pushed, we also remember what went on between us last time and can include such shared knowledge in our game – so it can be both predictable and the same, or different, every time.

The 'away!' game also addresses feelings of rejection and helplessness, always around with an autistic child. We want to get away, or feel the child wants us to go away. The game turns this around, by playing with our sense of being rejected and pushed away. At the same time it stimulates in the autistic child active and interactive elements of watching, listening and pushing, and eventually perhaps even vocalising and saying the word 'away' himself. These elements can then be applied in other situations in which he wants to express that he does not want something, for example during drinks time we may offer him, in a *playfully* pushy sort of way, something we know he does not like, with no other intention than to *enable him to push it away*, i.e. to say 'no'. Or we can offer him the obviously wrong hat, coat or shoe …

> Fred only drank orange juice. His key-worker knew that. So sometimes she offered him Ribena, just to give him the opportunity to say 'no'. She would hold the jug very still right in front of him, asking him, also with her eyes and smiling face, whether he wanted Ribena. He would push it

away with an angry, irritated gesture, which she put in words with an expressive '"NO!", says Fred, "take that *away!*"'

This game is not easy to teach, because getting the balance of the back-and-forth and the teasing right is crucial. This is dependent on the adult's intuitive sensitivity to each child. She has to be able to tune in to the individual child and aim her responses precisely at what this child does or does not like, can or cannot tolerate, and what their mutual relationship allows for. I had not seen two-year-old Mustafa for several weeks, and he clearly felt that he did not know me as well as I thought I knew him:

As a greeting I touched him lightly with my finger, saying 'That's *Mustafa.*' He 'looked daggers' at me and, shrinking away angrily, pushed my hand away. 'Away!' I said for him, trying to catch his angry face in my tone of voice. I had obviously violated his space and he felt intruded upon. I then held my hand near him again, wanting to acknowledge and replay what had just happened. He instantly pushed it away again with growing indignation. I said '"Away!", says Mustafa', holding my hand near him in quick succession for him to push away. He began to smile, and looked into my face as if in doubt about what on earth was happening – and his earlier hostility relaxed into a relieved, friendly smile.

Here the game established, or re-established, a relationship with a child after the adult's first approach had gone wrong and the child had somehow felt threatened. The speed of the repeated 'as if' intrusions of my hand, together with the fact that I did not touch him again, invalidated his initial sense of threat, leaving no other interpretation than that of shared playfulness.

One word of caution at the end. Because the described 'Away!' game plays with the theme of rejection, a very painful feeling, it can be in danger of inadvertently or unconsciously being abused or misused. All of us get hurt. All of us sometimes feel revengeful or hateful when we feel rejected or hurt too much. All of us have a little sadistic streak which needs keeping under control. Occasionally, we may not be aware of this shining through in what we do. Therefore, this game should only be played if the adult is firmly rooted, seeing things from the child's and a clearly playful perspective, which makes sure that adult and child will have as much fun as each other. Then it is great fun and a great one for encouraging communication in an autistic child.

5
Vocal and Musical Interaction Games

Mouth and Face Games: Play Music with Your Face

Our face and what I call 'Mouth and Face Games' have an important function in our attempts at helping the young autistic child to catch up with some of his developmental delay. Nothing more than larger-than-life elaborations of the earlier baby-babbling games of 'pure interaction', they aim to use whatever remnants of instinctive interest and responses there may be, to recreate face-to-face situations that are interactive, playful and fun. The baby's earliest vocabulary includes grunts, gurgles, shrieks, coughs, smacking his tongue or his lips, blowing raspberries, making bubbling and lots of other sounds, impossible to describe in words, but happily echoed by any tuned-in adult. They require no tools or equipment, just looking, listening, copying and echoing each other's sounds. All we need in our tool kit is our face, eyes and voice, a thoughtful and feelingful mind, an interest in careful observation, some sensitive awareness of our own pre-verbal communicative potential, a willingness to wait, watch and respond rather than to teach and demand, and to keep our concentration tightly focussed on the child's face and subtle communications.

'Pure interaction games' are the developmentally very early baby games which do not involve symbolic understanding. They can be played anywhere at any time and in between. Initiated by adult or child, they usually last only a few minutes or seconds, and many people are probably not even aware that they are playing them. What we are trying to recreate with the autistic child are such interactions as this between four-and-a-half month-old baby Joey and his mother:

> Joey is sitting on his mother's lap, facing her. She looks at him intently but with no expression on her face, as if she were preoccupied and

absorbed in thought elsewhere. At first, he glances at the different parts of her face but finally looks into her eyes. He and she remain locked in a silent mutual gaze for a long moment. She finally breaks it by easing into a slight smile. Joey quickly leans forward and returns her smile. They smile together; or rather they trade smiles back and forth several times. Then Joey's mother moves into a gamelike sequence. She opens her face into an expression of exaggerated surprise, leans all the way forward, and touches her nose to his, smiling and making bubbling sounds all the while. Joey explodes with delight but closes his eyes when their noses touch. She then reels back, pauses to increase the suspense, and sweeps forward again to touch noses. Her face and voice are even more full of delight and 'pretend' menace. This time Joey is both more tense and excited. His smile freezes. His expression moves back and forth between pleasure and fear. Joey's mother seems not to have noticed the change in him. After another suspenseful pause, she makes a third nose-to-nose approach at an even higher level of hilarity, and lets out a rousing 'oooOH!' Joey's face tightens. He closes his eyes and turns his head to the side. His mother realises that she has gone too far, and stops her end of the interaction, too. At least for a moment, she does nothing. Then she whispers to him and breaks into a warm smile. He becomes re-engaged. (Stern 1991)

Although Joey is actively seeking social and communicative contact, the success of the interaction is almost entirely dependent on his mother being exquisitly responsive to him in timing, intensity and content. Rather than expecting the baby to join in with what the adult wants to do, all baby games of early communication depend on the adult being responsive to what the baby is already doing, has done, is about to do. Joey's mother responds to what he is doing: in this case no more than seeking her attention. Due to Joey's perseverance, she finally notices his unspoken question and replies. He was not just looking *at* her, he was looking *for* her, and without words they play a question-and-answer game, have an argument, fall out, apologise, and make up again. When his mother goes too far, Joey cuts off and withdraws. In this example the adult uses nothing more sophisticated than simply waiting in silence, letting some suspense build up as a natural motivator, while keeping her attention tightly focussed on the child. She thus supports his drive for mastery and control, helps him regulate how much he can take, and to remain in touch with another person. When she whispers to him he is able to reconnect with her.

The idea of such baby interaction provides us with a mental model to help us when we want to draw the young autistic child, who may be watching out of the corner of his eyes, or ears, or not at all, into face-to-face communication. Unexpected, funny or unusual noises are especially suited to this, but the first 'attention catcher' is our breath: a sudden voiced in-breath, drawn in deeply, as when suddenly faced with the perhaps most shocking sight, is likely to get even the most withdrawn autistic child to look up at least for a split second. It plays on an instinctive startle reflex that both signals alarm and sends an instinctive warning message. It may take as much as this to 'startle' or 'kick-start' his hibernating mind into alertness, to where we can then meet it with the warmest or gentlest smile. Once we have 'caught' his attention, we want to hold this precious capacity, to stretch and extend it as far as it will go. This was more difficult with Tim than with Patrick:

> Tim was an expert in avoiding communicative encounters. If I faced him closely, at about 30cm and in his line or peripheral field of vision, making some noises with my mouth, he would simply sweep his eyes past my face and stare the other way. But if I then moved my face back a little, together with a noisy warning gasp, his eyes would follow the movement and we would be looking into each other's eyes, at least for a split second. If I *immediately* burst out into an exaggerated smiling 'greeting face' together with a surprised and extremely welcoming 'HellooOO?! Hello TIM!?!', I could hold his attention and interest for perhaps a few more split seconds. If I repeated this, making surprising and unexpected noises with my mouth, such as blowing raspberries, suddenly plopping my lips or wiggling my tongue quickly and noisily from side to side, he would watch with surprise. With slightly different variations each time, it was possible to stretch Tim's attention and to hold his interest for some minutes.

Minutes for Tim are a very long time compared with the fleeting split seconds which he has become used to. Normally, he seems incapable of such human connectedness and contact. But there were islands here of unexpected potential and possibilities. Could we help Tim to enlarge these islands, to expand the time and reduce the empty spaces in between? Could we show him that such face-to-face games are fun, and whet his appetite for more? Could we develop little routines of social 'mouth and face games', so he would come to *ask* for an interrupted game sequence to be completed?

> Patrick wasn't one for joining in. He had his own agenda. But finally he relented and sat down. Sitting opposite I made the most peculiar vocal noises I could. He looked up with sudden interest. I did it again, all my attention focussed on him, trying to hold his interest through the expressivity of my own face. Then I paused mid-way, to encourage him to take

over the sound-making himself, widening my eyes to show that my attention was still all on him, before offering a weaker version myself, anxious not to lose our hard-won 'shared attention'. And indeed, he tried to copy my 'raspberries'. I echoed him, and he did it again, this time with more 'umph'. After a few rounds, I added a tongue click, then waited for him to take his turn. He did. We were now having a dialogue game of 'raspberries – tongue click – : your turn!'. I added a vocal sound at the end, and Patrick copied this too. And then it was my turn to be surprised. Patrick's next turn went: 'raspberries' – tongue click – vocal sound – punch air and shout!' He looked at me with a broad grin. It was wonderful. Patrick had not only understood the idea of copying vocal sounds, but also the idea of sequencing and adding new elements. This was creative. We continued for about ten minutes, and only stopped because we had to. From then on, Patrick 'asked' daily for 'mouth and face games'.

We can make an infinite abundance of shapes and noises with our mouth, which can all be separately adjusted and fine-tuned according to each individual child. Each of us is like an orchestra of which we are the conductor. Many of the players we have never met, and most of us are unaware of a large section of our personal orchestra's potential – here are some of them:

We can speak, sing, hum, and make all sorts of sounds and noises with our *voice*, which has a wide range of volume, from totally soundless to loud-voiced whispering, from 'room temperature' volume to loud shouting-pitch. We can decrease and increase its volume, play around with speed and tempo: slow or fast, suddenly or gradually, or gradually at first and suddenly much faster, or louder, or vice versa – then suddenly stop or change modality. It has a wide range of pitch: we can speak or sing in a high voice or a deep one, growl, quack, miaow, bark, grunt, squeak, make vocal sounds that are funny, silly, surprising or even rude, from silly high-pitched ones like a mouse or a deep lion's roar. We can develop different rhythms, to be repeated or not. We can speak in a distinctive rap rhythm, sing what we want to say, or speak it to the rhythm of a particular favourite song. We can take a noisy in-*breath*, or sigh with an equally noisy out-breath. We can even make a *pretend* version of a dramatically exaggerated 'mock-shocked' gasp clearly different from one of more real shock, concern or alarm.

We can use our *mouth* to make silent shapes or funny noises like blowing raspberries, plopping our lips, smacking our tongue or lips. We can smile, laugh, giggle, grin, show our teeth, whistle in many different ways, high and low, long or short, loudly and quietly. We can stick out our tongue, wiggle it from side to side, up and down, in and out, with our mouth open or shut. It can pop out for the briefest peek-a-boo, disappear again only to pop unexpectedly out of the other corner of our mouth. We can blow up our cheeks, or just one, and suddenly let the air explode, disappear or pop out.

Our *face* is capable of expressing a huge range of emotions. We can widen or narrow our eyes, in real and pretend surprise, joy, fear, shock, amazement. We can frown, take up an 'attention-getting face', a 'greeting-face' or a pretend-cross one. We can pretend to cry, to be frightened, bored, appalled, or open our eyes and mouth wide with the most extreme pretend-amazement, 'make it bigger' fashion (see chapter 1).

We can use our *head* and *body* to increase or decrease distance. We can move just our head back, or our whole body, or get up and take a step back. We can move away and then suddenly swing back again, with our face only or our entire body, or just our hand. We can move further away than expected by just a tiny bit or a lot. We can come much closer than expected, but only for a split second. We can make as if we were to come close and touch him, and then suddenly stop and withdraw instead, or freeze in mid-motion, or mid-talking, or in the middle of being about to tickle him. We can freeze for a short moment and continue, or we can freeze in a pre-climax way for as long as it takes him to take his turn and look, or move, or make some sound in order to get us to continue. We can accompany all this by talking, singing – or ominous silence.

With our *hands* and *fingers* we can touch, stroke, point, pat, tap, tickle or finger-march up his arm or leg. We can use a 'wiggly worm' finger (see chapter 4) to create anticipation and a humorous giggly situation. We can clap, wave or hide our hands, snip our fingers – once and unexpectedly, or alongside the rhythm or tune we are singing. We can creak and squeak while moving our arms and hands like the robotic 'rap dances' of some youngsters in the streets. Last but not least there is of course also the wide communicative field of *emotional body language*.

With all these we try to (re-)create the most basic situation of 'shared attention'. Initially the adult will be copying the child's sounds, once he makes any, exactly and almost simultaneously, as with a baby. At the next level of communicative development, a little pause is left before echoing the child's sounds, exactly at first – with little variations with a child like Patrick, who has mastered the earlier stages. Throughout, the game is characterised by both players developing little routines together and rhythms of mouth-shapes, noises and gestures. Such familiar sequences set up expectations in the child, which, if sensitively used, can stir him into communicating what should be next:

> Once Patrick and I had developed a sequence of sounds and actions, we could each add bits for the other to copy. I also used two other 'tricks': often I would start, then pause suddenly, smiling expectantly. Or I might

make *as if* I was going to click my tongue, but then freeze with my tongue visibly in my mouth – which would invariably get him to finish or to put in the next bit of the sequence, like the tongue click.

At other times, I would get it wrong: playful 'messing up' often motivates a young child into communicative action. I'd start off alright, but then leave a bit out – and hesitate, for example 'raspberries' – vocal sound – punch air with right fist and – tongue click (instead of shout)'. Pretending to be surprised, when he 'corrected' me, I'd apologise (all in good humour) and start again from the beginning ... it's fun.

However, we must bear in mind throughout that although the autistic child may be able to, he is likely to be very unused to using his mind in such ways. His threshold for being over-stimulated by too much of anything, and to feel pushed over the edge, may be minute. Therefore, while one autistic child may need us to greet him with the broadest and warmest smile we have, another may need a much cooler version, like the faintest and most unobtrusive smile or look we have available. It is our responsibility as adults to *remain sensitive to the level of stimulation and frustration each child can tolerate at any given moment*, and to stop and tune down our efforts at the slightest sign of seeing him withdraw or get frightened. With normal babies we abandon ourselves to the joy of such social contact and mucking about. But with the autistic child we must be much more aware of what exactly we are doing, which precise elements attract, which subtle variations will maintain his attention, and which won't. He needs us to regulate these interactions for him, constantly adjusting the 'temperature' and intensity of our encounters to fit his variable and hypersensitive tolerances. In order to sustain his interest and delight, we need to try not to transgress his tolerance for frustration and to concentrate on an 'optimal range' band of interaction without letting it become rigid, lifeless, and boring.

However, as we are human, fallible and prone to making mistakes, despite trying not to transgress this will happen naturally through little mistunings and mismatches. These have their place too, as we saw in the example of Joey. The stuff of human relationships and communication, they help to keep things alive. But balancing this is like tightrope walking. It requires much patient perseverance, great attention to detail and determination. If you make sure that things remain definitely playful, by smiling broadly, with the very occasional tickle perhaps to enliven his flagging life-spirits, and using a dramatic tone of voice, pulling all the registers from softest to louder and higher pitched, from slow to faster and then – suddenly – : 'plop!' with your lips, then even the most autistic child won't be able to resist looking in your face. At that moment, we want to use our intuition to sense how each child feels about the world, what he or she enjoys or finds (too) scary, and to amplify whatever there is with a certain laid-back and relaxed confidence, a definite sense of humour, playfulness and fun, much empathy and understanding, while being aware that we are with a very much younger person (developmentally speaking). In this way we will be able to meet him on his level to invite him into some 'fun and games' of human interaction.

Pointing is a Child's First Sentence: From Shared Attention to Learning to Talk

Autistic children do not point with their index finger as every one-year-old does, and a lack of pointing is seen as an important diagnostic criterion for autism. Recent research suggests that pointing is crucial for the development of language, and that children do not learn to speak until they have understood the meaning of pointing things out to someone (Newson 1999). But pointing is much more than what one does with one's index finger. Pointing is really a child's first sentence: an early pre-verbal form of naming. Meaningful language relies on the shared attention between two people. Pointing at something for someone else to see is the earliest expression of this desire to share with another person what we see, think or want the other to know about. Meaningful speech and language can only develop if this kind of pre-verbal communication has been sufficiently practised.

There are two main kinds of 'pointing-sentences': one points at something and says 'I want that' (proto-imperative pointing'), and most autistic children do do this kind of pointing, although it is often more of a grabbing gesture with their hand than pointing with a single finger. Generally it is a toy or object they want to have or, frequently, something to eat. It is also usually accompanied by impatience and the demand to have whatever it is NOW. The autistic child is most likely to go himself to try to get at that out-of-reach biscuit on top of the cupboard with an unstoppable determination and persistence, rather than ask for help from another person by pointing to what he wants. This inability to wait is a major distinguishing feature of this first kind of pointing.

The second kind of pointing differentiates the autistic from the non-autistic child: it points at something with a carefully singled-out index finger as if to say 'Look! Can you see what I am looking at? I don't want to have it, I just want you to *know* about it' ('proto-declarative pointing'). The pointing is to help the other person follow the pointer's line of vision and to understand what it is he is looking at. It implies a lot of mental activity, understanding and empathy with the other person. It shows much more patience and there is no grabbing. The child does not want to have it, eat it, or take it away. All he wants is to tell you about it, for you to see and share with him what he is pointing out. He gets real enjoyment from hearing his pointing gesture summed up in words, for example 'Oh, yes, Nicki can see a bird', or 'Yes, crisps. On the bill-board. I can see it too', or 'Yes, you are right, there's a cat outside chasing the pigeons.' In response, the child beams with delight because you have understood, or grumbles and strains because this is not what he had in mind, that he was pointing out something different.

By about nine months, a baby normally understands that he can 'have' something by having it in his mind, and so can other people. Mummy, for example, has a mind and he knows that she knows what he likes, what he knows, what he is interested in and is likely to want. When he points out of the window, he looks back to check her eyes, to see that she is looking up into the sky too. If she is looking down at the pigeons on the ground instead, he corrects her with demanding noises until she follows his finger- and eye-point. Autistic children cannot, or do not, do this, although some 'eye-point' with their eyes by looking at what they 'have their eye on', which may be a beginning of pointing.

Recent research suggests that the gesture of pointing only seems to occur in children who have developed 'pincer-grip', i.e. the ability to pick up small objects, like a raisin or a grain of rice, with their thumb and index finger. Children who develop pincer-grip late are also late in pointing at things. This implies that a child has to learn first to single out and focus on a small object which he wants to pick up, and then to coordinate and match what he has in mind with his fine-motor skills. Pointing at things that are further away seems to be the next developmental step. It indicates a form of mental reaching out and taking in, almost as if taking the other person *mentally* by the hand to lead them, by the symbolic gesture of a minimised or 'atrophied' hand, visually to what is being pointed out. When we use words, it is as if we were pointing *verbally* at what we mean, and in writing this I am pointing out something in my mind to the reader, who understands when his or her eyes 'point' to the words on this page.

Being able to take in with eyes and mind, to keep something in mind, and to be able to bear the frustration of not actually having, touching, grabbing, possessing, eating it, means that the child needs to be able to tolerate the object being at a distance, and to be confident about being able to bridge that distance mentally by communicating. Such confidence requires a good deal of frustration tolerance, the ability to wait and being willing to negotiate with another person: not most autistic children's greatest strengths.

Whether it is possible to actually teach someone how to point, I don't know. Pointing seems to develop naturally, as a baby's communicative development and his understanding of its functions matures. If he is not yet ready, then singling out his finger into a pointing gesture may be in vain – but then it may not be. Any activities that encourage a poking gesture with one finger may be a possible beginning.

A sequencing activity of asking the child to push bits of cotton-wool, beads, raisins, etc., into holes cut into an upside-down egg carton, then picking them up with pincer-grip could teach him a form of early turn-taking, sequencing, some waiting – and perhaps also something like a pointing gesture.

But while it may be difficult (or impossible) to teach him to point, we can certainly make an effort to show him its uses by repeatedly pointing out things we know he is interested in. Situations in which it is impossible to actually *have* what is being pointed out are particularly useful, as they invite him to pay attention mentally, without the temptation to grab, have and eat whatever it is. The easiest situations for this are outdoors and with picture books.

If she does not resist too much, we may take the child's pointing-finger into our hand and point out with it something exciting like 'Look! There's a computer in the picture. Leila likes the computer', the 'Look!' said in a tone of great surprise, as if we had just seen the most exciting sight of our lives.

We can emphatically point out something the child is already looking at with an exaggerated 'Look! A plane', even if we think that he will never understand what we are saying or pointing at. If we use a dramatic enough tone of voice and gestures, without being threatening, he will be unable to resist looking (watch his face and bodily reactions for this). If you think that perhaps he did feel threatened, try again with the same 'dramatic-ness' but whispered. If this fails try again with your voice at 'room temperature' but at a distance of 1 foot or more. If this also fails try it whispered at 3 feet. Keep trying. At least he may get the idea that we are *trying* – and it keeps him 'live company'. It also keeps our morale going, which is almost as important.

The moment he looks at what we are pointing out to him, we have achieved a moment of our big aim of 'shared attention', so necessary for real communication. He may still not be able to initiate it, but being able to follow and focus on our finger, and to join with what we are looking at and showing him, is a first step. We may need to keep 'calling' his attention to an object of interest again and again, and it may be a huge effort every time. But at least it'll give him some practice.

Before giving him something, like a biscuit or his coat before going out, we can also make a conscious effort to stop at some distance from the desired object and point to what *the child* (not the adult, that would be much too complicated) wants – again, in the most dramatic and exaggerated ways of 'making it bigger', in fact, as big as we can. If *we* follow what he wants, what he is already looking at, then we already have that aimed-for 'shared attention', i.e. seeing and thinking of the same object for a moment. With the child who can and likes to copy actions, we can also sing songs that include the pointing gesture, like 'Peter Pointer', or songs made up for that purpose.

Songs that Work and Why: Action Songs, Zappy Rhythms and Surprises

Not only is singing fun, it is also our most important tool for helping the young autistic child to catch up with some of his communicative developmental delay. But some songs simply do not seem to 'work' with the autistic child, i.e. songs that involve imagination, or depend on understanding the meaning of words and language. This includes songs which are *not* action songs, such as 'Baa Baa Black Sheep', 'Oranges and Lemons', 'Old MacDonald', and lots of other well-known children's songs, except if their tunes are used for running-commentary songs. Other songs work extremely well, and I have seen several autistic children first attempt to make sounds, or even say words, within the context of one of these familiar songs. A song 'works' if it captivates the child's attention enough for him to be willing to sit down, join in, remember and 'ask' for it again.

The factors that promise to make a song successful in attracting and holding the young pre-verbal child's attention and interest, whether a baby of eight months or an autistic child of four years, are:

1. lots of actions that give him something to do,
2. a zappy, lively, exciting rhythm that gets into his blood, and
3. suspense and excitement-generating anticipation to grab and hold his attention.

Because of his difficulty with language and meaning, what is important for the autistic child are the rhythm and tune, not the words or story of a song. This requires rethinking and relistening to songs for many adults: which songs do you know which have a catchy, exciting, stimulating and enlivening tune and rhythm, never mind the words? And which songs thrive on the words or story-line with a less catchy tune? Concentrate on the first lot.

The words of a song have most chance of catching his attention, if they are combined with definite gestures or actions. Quiet, sad, slow or thoughtful songs like 'Twinkle Twinkle Little Star' are often not very successful in getting the autistic child to join in, because not enough is happening in them to keep him interested. Their subdued mood does not excite or hold his attention, it fails to get into his blood and to rouse his interest, which means he is likely to wander or to switch off.

Songs that require cooperation tend to fall flat, such as two children having to hold hands to dance together, as many younger children resist the idea of holding someone else's hands and having theirs held. Others like it 'being done to them' by an adult, but will not participate actively. The second 'verse' of this song has, however, much greater potential for getting the autistic child to join in, once he knows the routine, provided the adult can wait long enough, stretching out the suspense as long as possible – until the imaginary elastic is about to snap and the child himself makes some contribution towards the scream:

1a. Row row **row your boat**
    Gently down the stream,
    Merrily, merrily, merrily, merrily,
    Life is but a dream.

b. Row row row your boat
    Gently down the stream,
    And if you meet a crocodile
    Don't forget to ... **scream:** ...
    aaahhh!!

The circle song 'Ring a Ring a Roses' usually works if there are enough adults and cooperative children to facilitate the holding of hands – otherwise the autistic child wanders off into less socially demanding corners of the room, making himself miss out on an activity he does in fact enjoy. But most of them love circle games, especially those 'playing with distance' by going in and out, like 'Hokey Cokey', a useful song because new verses and actions can easily be added. I once knew some nursery workers who got terribly worried that the autistic child would find 'right' and 'left' confusing. But because every child, even the most autistic, will have a sense of 'one and then the other', what adults call them doesn't matter, as putting one foot, or arm 'in', and then the other, is perfectly understandable to anyone. And whether anyone gets it right or wrong does not really make that much difference. The advantage of using left and right is that it gives the song enough length to build up a good measure of anticipation and suspense (if you see to that!), until you can 'put your whole self in', which means jumping in and out, which all children love.

2. **Hokey Cokey:**
You put your left foot in, your left foot out,
in, out, in, out, you shake it all about.
You do the hokey cokey

and you turn around.
That's what it's all about.
Oooooh, hokey cokey cokey! [everyone going into centre]
Oooooh, hokey cokey cokey! [moving as far out as your arms will stretch]
Knees bent, arms up, ra ra ra [meaning: clap clap clap]!
(... right foot, left arm, right arm, bum, head, whole self; left side, right side;
elbow, knee, toe, nose, left ear, right ear ...)

While working on such circle songs with certain children is appropriate, it
is helpful to keep in mind that from a developmental point of view cooperative behaviour comes after, not before or instead of, the very early
communicative interest in the other person's facial expressions and wanting
to show things by pointing and sharing the knowledge of this in 'joint
attention'. This developmental aim is best met in those rhymes that depend
heavily on suspense and facial expressions, for example 'Here's the Beehive',
'Five Peas', 'Round and Round the Garden':

3a. **Here is the beehive**, where are   b. **Here is my hand**, but my
    the bees?   fingers: where are they?
    Hiding away where nobody sees!   In my fist they're hiding away!
    Here they come creeping   Out they come, fit and alive:
    out of their hive,   1 – 2 – 3, 4, ...5 ....:
    1 – 2 – 3, 4, ...5 ....:   There!(or: Got you!)!!!
    bzzzzzzzzzz!!!

4a. **Five peas** in a peapod pressed,   b. **Five fingers** held tight in one fist,
    one grew, two grew,   One crept out, another crept out,
    and so did all the rest.   and the last one's not to be missed.
    They grew and they grew   They wriggled about
    and they could not stop,   in Jazzy's lap,
    until one day the pod went   until all of a sudden Jazzy's
    ....'POP'!   hands went 'CLAP'!

5. **Round and round the garden**
    like a teddy bear.
    1 step, 2 steps, ...:
    tickle you under there!

And remember, that once you have found a tune or rhythm that works,
you can add any words you like. There is no law to say we are not allowed
to be creative and invent our own verses to a tune. People don't often think
of this. Most of us are not musicians or composers. But all of us can put our
own words to a familiar tune.

6. **This little boy** went to nursery,
   this little boy stayed home.
   This little boy had biscuits,
   this little boy had none,
   and this little boy cried wahahaha all the way home.

7. **Up and down**, up and down,
   out and in, out and in,
   from side to side, from side to side,
   and here we go again:
   Ready – aaaand – (faster, louder, whispering, crying, laughing, angry, ...)
   Up and down, ...

Some circle songs, such as the 'Up and down' song, are intended for a group of children holding hands, brilliant for building up anticipation and suspense to hold their attention. It is among the best action songs to coax the non-verbal autistic child into making a sound – provided you can manage to wait long enough after 'ready – and –', with everyone's hands suspended in mid-air, until some child can tolerate it no longer and volunteers 'UP!' for the game to continue.

> The 'Up and down' song, so simple and direct that it can be 'played' with even the most withdrawn autistic child, was one of the first ways in which I was able to make contact with Derek, who at that time had developed a habit of lying around on the floor. Kneeling beside him, or perhaps playfully standing over him, I would move his arms, or legs, up and down, from side to side, in and out with the tune. Soon I was able to stop, as if the process or song had got stuck, looking at him with big eyes and waiting expectantly for him to 'get the ball rolling again' by making some sound or movement, or by looking at me, to get me to continue singing and moving his arms or legs. Once he knew the song from our one-to-one games, he was much more motivated to join in with it in a group setting.

Any song or nursery rhyme that can be made to include an element of suspense and surprise, that can be stretched and extended to such an enormous extent that it virtually *commands* the attention of even the most gone-astray or cut-off child, will be a success. Some songs have a definite catchy end, perhaps with a tickle or a somewhat unexpected 'clap' or bounce on the adult's knee, so we can make maximum use of dramatic pauses and anticipation as the most powerful attention-getters, for example 'Here is the Beehive', 'Five peas', 'Chick chick chicken', 'Derek's on Mary's knee', ...

8a. **Chick chick chick chick chicken,** lay a little egg for me.
   Chick chick chick chick chicken, a brown one for my tea.
   Oh, I haven't had one since breakfast, and now its half-past three, hey!
   Chick chick chick chick chicken, lay a little egg for me
8b. Trip trip trip trip-tree-ee, who is this with me?
   Trip trip trip trip-tree-ee, who is on my knee?
   Oh, it's Derek on my knee here,
   he's going up and down, – weeh!
   Trip trip trip trip-tree-ee, it's Derek on my knee!

A catchy, stimulating, alerting, zappy, lively, springy, cheerful tune often has dotted notes, a syncopated and very accentuated pulse or rhythm, unexpected pauses, crescendos or decrescendos, and other musical elements, that go against the expected harmonies: music that stimulates, that jars us into listening, that leaves us completely at sea as to where the downbeat is, as if on the high point of a roller-coaster. This is what makes it exciting. A tune that has swing, that really pushes and pulls the notes, as in a Samba or a Waltz, in Salsa or African, Irish or Latin American (to name but a few) music, or a tune that is very off-beat, gives you a thrill, as if your heart has missed a beat – the more abdominal the better, and usually with a rhythm faster than the normal heartbeat.

Action songs with a continuous flow of changing actions to accompany the singing tend to be most successful, especially those with simple non-symbolic actions involving body parts, as in 'Head, Shoulders, Knees and Toes', 'Roly Poly Poly Up and Down', ... and the first part of 'Wind the Bobbin Up' (which loses most autistic children when it comes to pointing with one finger though we can use it to try teaching them to point). We can:

clap	– hands
shake	– hands, head, feet, arms, legs
stamp	– feet
nod	– head
stretch	– arms up/ down, side to side, left and right, forward and back
shake	– hands, head, feet, arms, legs
click	– fingers, tongue,
blink	– eyes
tap	– knee, elbow, nose, chin, cheek, head, foot, toe, leg, ...; floor, chair, ...
touch, rub, point to	– ear, nose, teeth, tummy, eye, mouth, hair, head, chest, arm, elbow, knee, leg, foot, toe, shoulder, ...; floor, chair, ceiling, ...

wobble	– whole body, mouth
wiggle	– finger, tongue,
clatter	– teeth

9a. **Head, shoulders, knees and toes, knees and toes,** (2x) and
eyes and ears and mouth and nose,
Head , shoulders, knees and toes, knees and toes!

9b. **Teeth, elbows, thighs and neck, thighs and neck,** (2x) and
forehead, chin, tongue, hair and back,
teeth, elbows, thighs and neck, thighs and neck!

10a. **Roly poly** poly poly up and down, (3x)
now put your hands together 1, 2, 3!
10b. Shakey-shakey-shakey shakey side to side (3x)
now put your hands together 1, 2, 3!
10c. Wibble wobble (2x) forwards and back (body)
10d. Left and right (2x) and nod nod nod (head)
10e. In and out (2x) and stamp stamp stamp (feet on floor)
10f. Open, shut them, (2x) blink blink blink (eyes) etc.

11. **Wind the bobbin up** (2x)
Pull! Pull! Clap clap clap!
Point to the ceiling, point to the floor,
point to the window, point to the door!
Put your hands together, 1, 2, 3,
put your hands upon your knees!

'Running commentary songs' (see chapter 2) are incredibly useful with the
autistic child: they liven things up, keep us company, create a sense of
togetherness and contact, when there's no response when talking to him.
Any tune can be used, with the simpler ones being easier to find words for:

12. (to the tune of 'Here we go round the Mulberry Bush'):
This is the way Jason puts on his coat (socks, shoes, jumper, trousers;
pulls down his jumper, ...)
puts on his coat (2x)
This is the way Jason puts on his coat,
on a rainy Thursday morning.

13. (to the tune of 'The wheels on the bus'):
    Now we are going to put on our socks, put on our socks, put on our socks,
    and now we are going to put on our socks – and pull them up!
    (put on shoes, trousers, ... tidy up toys, put them in the box, ... roll the ball, the car, ... wash hands, brush teeth, sit down, bring a chair, ... draw a picture, scribble with the pen, ... jump up and down, ...)

14. (to the tune of 'If you're happy and you know it clap your hands'):
    If we want to we can clap our hands (2x)
    If we want to we can clap our hands like this,
    If we want to we can clap our hands.
    (stamp our feet, nod our head, scratch our nose, shake your hands, rub your tummy, ...)

As always there is the risk that some of the autistic mental functioning may rub off on the adults. In one nursery the adults were so worried about making a mistake with the new songs that they put them up in big letters on the wall – with the result that three years later none of the adults knew the words by heart. Every day before dinner they sang the same songs, reading them off the wall. But once the song has been sung a few times, making a mistake provides true communicative opportunities: often a child who does not usually use his voice to communicate will surprise us by correcting us with what we *should* have said, or sung! So give him a chance by making mistakes!

It does not have to be neat rhymes – any words that make sense (or not: many old nursery rhymes do not make much sense as it is!) will do fine, as long as they keep you and the child, the song and the tune going! Sometimes it is worth carefully making up words to fit a tune and particular child (such as my attempt with my new verse of 'I'm a Little Teapot'). But often any kind of improvisation will do. Sometimes you may have to squash several syllables together, which may, in fact, even alert the autistic child to the meaning of the words: although the tune stays the same, it gets slightly 'messed up' because of the words.

All in all, the usefulness of singing and using tunes with an autistic child cannot be stressed enough. We want to pick those songs with the most power to attract and hold his attention and interest, which means that they must have a zappy, lively, exciting rhythm that gets into his blood, and lots of actions, that give him something to do, to help him focus. The more suspense and excitement-generating anticipation there is, the more chance for his flagging attention to be grabbed and jolted again. Because of his lack of imagination and interest in symbolic meanings, actions to do with his own body are most successful. This also encourages the autistic child to watch and copy what you are doing, thus engaging in some form of inter-active activity. 'Running commentary songs' can be made from any song you or the child like, adding your own words to suit the situation. In this way you can virtually sing yourself through the entire day.

6
Interaction Games using Toys, Books and other Objects

Peekaboo and Hiding Games:
Attention and Interaction through Suspense and Surprise

All young children love peekaboo games. Driven by instinctive responses of anticipation and excitement within a clear rule structure, they are crucial for language development and social awareness. The earliest version of peekaboo games is the 'looming game' in which an adult approaches a young baby from a distance of about a metre, then looms towards him so their faces almost touch (Bruner 1976). In a 'looming game' the adult is usually looking down at a baby gazing up at her face (see chapter 1). With the basic rules the same, this version is often successful with more passive autistic children.

Despite the autistic child's developmental delay, his instinctive responses are usually unimpaired, provided the stimulus is strong, sensitively attuned, playful and non-threatening enough. Any activity that invites him into social interaction strengthens the growth of his communicative non-autistic potential, especially if it involves face-to-face contact. If this contact is so much fun that he is motivated to seek out such situations voluntarily, then he is doing something profoundly non-autistic, because it is more fun than his usual solitary or repetitive activities. Autistic children also need help to focus their attention, stretch their concentration span, learn to wait for and take turns, and watch for the other person's response. Peekaboo games score highly on all of these. They also encourage a sense of humour, a complex achievement in terms of social skills, communication, the boundary between 'real' and 'make-believe', i.e. the earliest beginnings of pretend-play and symbolisation.

A peekaboo game always starts with an opening move, in which both players make explicit contact with each other, usually by looking at each other face to face, however briefly. Where this does not occur, the adult may initate this with a dramatic in-breath or an excitement-generating 'hello!?' At other times, we can attract the child's attention by making the 'hiding instrument' very obvious or interesting, for example 'wiggling' the blanket, scarf, cardigan or book we are using to hide behind, suddenly lifting it up high, or moving it quickly to one side or the other, across his field of vision. The purpose of this introductory mutual attention-focussing episode is to arouse his curiosity, to focus his attention, and to confirm that each player is aware of the other. It contains an unspoken agreement that this game is played for no other reason than to be social and have fun together.

The game follows certain rules, and the child comes to expect disappearance and reappearance in a particular place, at a particular time, in a particular situation, accompanied by particular vocal sounds. Playing around with these expectancies determines the success of the game. Waiting and not knowing when, where, and how the face will reappear builds up suspense and exciting tension. Once the game is set up, its rules can be stretched and played with in endless variations.

Any chance event can be used as a starter for a spontaneous round of peekaboo, for example when a child's face is accidentally hidden while getting dressed by a jumper, a book, a toy, or your sleeve. It can be played with a blanket or a scarf that is large enough to cover both your heads, a good way to establish contact: you can both get under it together, which encourages eye contact as there are no visual distractions. You, or the child, may hide behind a door, a chair or a curtain, and either of you may have intended this to become a peekaboo game or not. It is each player's openness and willingness to allow events to unfold spontaneously that makes the game interesting, enjoyable and creative. Above all it is a game in which no mistake can be made. There is no failure, no wrong move. Any movement, sound, gesture, or the absence of any of these, simply becomes the next successful move in the game – the more unexpected the better.

Their teacher had brought a box with hats and wigs to her class of young autistic children to encourage eye contact and turn-taking. Children and adults were swapping hats and putting them onto each other's heads. Mohamed let all this happen without much interest or involvement until I pulled out a wig with long curly hair. With my face at his eye-level I swept it past his eyes to catch his attention and, covering my face, I slowly lifted it up over my nose and eyes to reveal my face.

He erupted into a broad grin, the quality of his looking changed and it was as if all of him had clicked into an altogether different gear: suddenly he seemed to see and recognise me, as if for the first time. And then he laughed. He laughed and giggled, looking at my eyes and face, reaching with his fingers to touch it, just like a much younger baby would do. I took the wig off, talking and laughing with him. He put it back on. After several rounds, I took it off, put it on his head and gave him a mirror. He looked at his image with smiling amazement. Then he turned and put the wig back on my head. I took it off and put it on another adult's head. He was delighted, looking with interest back and forth between the other adult and me. From that moment, we were strangers no longer, we were friends.

This was a dramatic moment of 'reclamation' of a child who had been lost somewhere in outer space. At first Mohamed seemed indifferent and apathetic, his eyes apparently unseeing, his attention unfocussed. But suddenly something in my face made his attention zoom into one meaningful focus, and he enjoyed our shared game tremendously.

The second round of peekaboo is the actual act of hiding, and all that goes with it. There are four basic alternatives: it can be the adult who is hidden or the child – with the hiding initiated either by the child or the adult. The two partners can stay in the same role, or one partner can suddenly 'refuse' to continue in their initial role, which 'forces' the other person to change roles and make the next communicative move themselves, if the game is to continue. As nothing is to be lost or gained, and nothing is at stake other than some social excitement and having fun with each other, the child will usually want to continue the game. He will, therefore, happily take the initiative to make the next communicative move. At that moment, a normally non-communicating child has chosen to make a spontaneous communication that has no other purpose than to continue a purely social game, just because he is enjoying it. As there is considerable release of tension, laughter particularly accompanies the moment of reappearance, thus creating a playful and enjoyable shared situation.

Partners can change roles, being the hiding one or the audience, covering their own face or the other person's, waiting for the other to pull the cover off, or pulling it off themselves. Different situations work with different children. If scarves are used, they could be made of different materials, such as dark and dense cloth or light see-through silks. We can alternate between textures, use scarves of different colours to make the world look yellow, pink or purple. We can even store each scarf with a different scent (a lavender or rose-petal pouch, a piece of sandal- or cedarwood, a minty chewing-gum, a cinnamon stick, some cloves) to give it additional intersensory interest (see chapter 8).

Timing is what makes or breaks the game, and it is through mindful use of timing that the adult can catch, hold, extend and channel the child's attention and concentration. The timing of the hiding and revealing can also change between turns. The face can reappear very quickly, very suddenly or very (even excruciatingly?) slowly. The hiding too can happen very suddenly, or very slowly. The adult can begin to hide without completing the hiding-act or 'tempt' the child by uncovering just a bit of her face, or perhaps just one eye, to prompt him to complete the action, i.e. to cooperate in a social interaction. If he wants the game to continue strongly enough, he is likely to communicate that he wants the adult to stop stalling the game. Such a communicative message from a child, who is not usually interested in socialising, depends on the adult's awareness of the game's communicative potential, her ability to wait patiently for much longer than she might expect to, and to create situations that require him to take the initiative. You need to experiment with waiting, holding the arch of suspense between you until he eventually does respond, without butting in yourself.

When the reappearance of a face is varied unexpectedly, suddenly popping up in a different place or position, he will be thrilled. At such moments his attention, should it have strayed, is firmly pulled back together into one single-minded focus. The constant variation within the game keeps enough uncertainty going to keep him mentally 'on his toes', which can be prolonged as his concentration span increases. After the hiding and peekaboo game described above, Mohamed 'asked' repeatedly for others to play such games with him again.

A successful round of peekaboo not only depends on the reappearance of a face, but also on the interesting sounds the adult makes throughout. The less familiar the game or the situation in which the game is played are to the child, the more important the sounds the adult makes seem to be. There is no limit to the variation of sounds, voiced breaths, and vocalisation on uncovering: the dramatic facial expressions and intonations an adult uses to attract a young child's attention, or larger-than-life voiced breaths, and sighs, and 'mock-shocked' in-breaths. The more common sounds on reappearance are 'boo!', 'there!', 'there he is!', but we could also say 'hello!', 'ahh!', 'there you are!', 'there's Tim!', or 'Got you!', and one could try to come up with a slightly new version every week, and then vary unexpectedly between these, to keep things alive.

There is, of course, always the possibility that an extremely sensitive child may become scared, because he is unable either to bear the tension of the excitement, or to differentiate between what is a real and what a playful pretend-threat. Some children react with a real or incipient avoidance response, when the loom is directly towards their face. This is a response with a healthy potential, as it can be the beginning of the child learning to say 'no!', 'stop it!', 'that is too much for me!' As adults we need to be attuned and responsive to each child's individual preference and tolerance-level, sensitively adapting our actions of looming, hiding and attention-getting, as well as our intonation, distance, speed of movement and speech, all intricately balanced to wherever the threshold of this particular child lies. Some children might need a louder or faster approach to gain and hold their interest, others need you to almost whisper and touch them as lightly as angels' hair to catch their attention. But that does not mean that they would not enjoy the game were it attuned just right. Keeping their activation level at an appropriate intensity needs constant adult monitoring.

Failures and serious problems in the game can be observed when an adult starts the game without having enlisted the child's attention first, or when the adult takes the cloth away from the child, rather than waiting or helping the child to do it himself. In such a case the adult is actually taking away the child's initiative, perhaps in an attempt to teach him how to do it. But a child cannot be taught, he can only be encouraged to learn; he needs us to provide him with opportunities to learn, not to provide ourselves with opportunities to teach.

Kofi liked peekaboo games. They were almost the only games he liked. His key-worker therefore often brought a scarf to play peekaboo with him. But Kofi was slow to respond, and not used to taking the initiative himself. When playing peekaboo the key-worker would pull off the scarf too quickly, without giving Kofi a chance to find out that he could actually do it himself. It did indeed require the adult to wait for what felt like an eternity for Kofi to come to life and to pull off the scarf. He seemed to do everything in slow motion. But he could do it! And Kofi's satisfied rare smile that went with it was definitely well worth the wait!

The principles that are fundamental to the successful game of peekaboo can also be applied and generalised to other hiding games, with dramatic hiding and revelation of whatever it is that has been hidden, like a sock in a shoe, a toy, a book, a biscuit. While such hide-and-seek is also accompanied by exaggerated facial expressions, dramatic breaths and sounds, this represents the next developmental step of sharing play and attention with another person.

The Meaning and Magic of Posting-boxes: 'This into That', 'There and Gone' and 'I Can Do It!'

My work with autistic and non-autistic young children has convinced me that the good old posting-box has much more hidden potential than is generally recognised. Normally regarded as an old-fashioned teaching toy for the cognitive development of shape recognition in babies, it has in fact unequalled powers to comfort a desperate young child and to help him master some early anxieties. Give a posting-box to an upset young child and help him post one shape at a time and he will usually settle down happily to an activity that gives him a sense of containment. He seems to derive a great sense of satisfaction from the fact that each shape has a 'home' it fits into *just so*, that there is a 'shape-answer' to each hole, a clearly organised system of things neatly fitting into each other, of 'this into that'. With autistic and developmentally delayed children, interest in posting-boxes is often a sign of a major developmental shift and cognitive–emotional progress.

The child who was helped most dramatically by a posting-box was Leila, screaming inconsolably again one day. I was struck by the image of the gaping hole of her wide open mouth expressing feelings of utter desolation. I thought about what a baby in this state would need and the underlying principle of his search for a sense of containment. I knew that if we gave Leila her bottle, she would happily plug herself up with it. I wondered what I could give her that would fulfil the same *mental–emotional function* without involving her mouth:

> I gave her a small posting-box with just one hole in it, that of a star, which I knew from quieter times to be her favourite posting-box shape. Immediately she went quiet, eagerly fitting the yellow and blue star shapes into the 'gaping hole'. Together we retrieved them, she posted them again, retrieved them, posted them, ... She then hid the box with both shapes inside behind my back, clung to me quietly for some moments, before climbing down to join the others for drinks.

Leila had been 'beside herself' with distress. I believe that it was the experience of the perfect fit between the hole and the shape, of *'that's* where it goes!', of 'this into that', of 'it fits *just so*' (this was my running commentary with which I tried to catch her emotional experience) that had managed to pull her together again like scattered iron filings by a magnet – a familiar situation with a fractious baby when finally put to the breast:

> Jenny was three months and lying on her back by herself next to her mother who was engrossed in a magazine and not paying attention to her. Her nose was blocked and she could not breathe well, which seemed to 'freak her out'. She grizzled, made vocal sounds, kicked her legs, waved her arms, then 'lost' it and began to cry bitterly. Carrying her around, letting her see the world from a different perspective, talking to her and holding her in different positions, helped a little. But when her mother

finally put Jenny to her breast (although she had just had a bottle and could not be hungry), the change was dramatic: suddenly this baby, who had seemed 'all over the place', was 'in one piece' again. Calm and quiet, sucking in a steady rhythm, Jenny's snuffliness was gone and she was breathing slowly and deeply. After a while, she stopped and looked at her mother, smiling.

Finding the nipple helped Jenny to literally 'pull herself together' in such a way that her breathing problems stopped, because all her senses and attention had become focussed by her mother's breast. Having got herself together again, she tried to make eye contact with her mother, almost as if to say 'thank you'. The experience of finding something that 'just fits', like the nipple that fills her mouth and stops her anxious feeling of franticness, must have been such a relief to Jenny. It was this scenario I had in mind when thinking how to help Leila. Whatever it was, it worked. For weeks, the star-posting-box went everywhere with us. It seemed to 'fix' her every time she came 'undone'.

Max's teachers were desperate: several times a day, Max screamed and nothing and no one could comfort him. What could they do? His mother brought him and left. He wandered around screaming, his bottle hanging from his mouth. I watched, as he swept toys to the floor, table after table. His destructive activity felt like a communication about what he was feeling inside: as scattered, uncontained and 'all over the place' as he was making his environment look. I searched for a posting-box, put the shapes in a bowl, so they wouldn't look scattered, and placing it on his lap, I handed him one shape next to its rightful 'home': he stopped screaming and pushed it in. 'Yes, that's where it goes: this into that!', I said offering him another one. He posted this too, trying the first hole first. 'No', I said, 'that's not where it goes. It's a *different* one. *That's* where it goes!', pointing to the correct hole. Handing him piece by piece, I encouraged him increasingly with my voice and words, rather than showing him with my fingers, to encourage him to listen and use his own mind. His teachers could not believe Max was quietly focussed on a task for such a long time.

Max had just been dropped off by his mother. His behaviour said 'I am in pieces'. His swiping toys off all the tables made the nursery room look as if someone had dropped a Lego structure which had shattered into pieces all over the place. Max too seemed 'all over the place'. When given the posting-box, it was now he himself who initiated the leaving and the finding: making the shapes disappear, just as his mummy had disappeared through the door. But now he could make them also reappear, just as he wished he could with his mum.

When Fred was struggling to let his father leave without disintegrating into despair, he played 'there and gone' by tossing a small red ball. One day, he saw someone with a posting-box and grabbed it urgently. The desperate quality with which he pulled it out of the adult's hand, and the absorbed total attention with which he concentrated on doing it again and again, suggested that it meant much more to Fred than just a cognitive activity he had outgrown.

Posting the shapes helped Fred work through some of his difficulties with letting go. It mirrored his emotional experience, and allowed him to develop mental structures to deal with the idea in his mind that Dad still exists even when Fred cannot see him, and that he will be able to 'retrieve' him again, as with the shapes (i.e. object-permanence).

With a posting-box it is the child who decides when to make something disappear, to go 'in' or 'come back', whether triangle, star, round shape, or in Fred's case: Daddy. Posting-boxes play with the theme of 'there and gone – and *there* again!', the greatest developmental issue to deal with for a child at the mental age of around one year. The issues that preoccupy a very young child are, above all, whether or not his most important people, and things, disappear, where to, whether or not they will come back, what he can do about it and how to deal with his feelings of anxiety and rage. Seeing Mummy, or Daddy, disappear is a painful and frightening experience. If he could do something about it, if he could somehow feel he had some control over it, it would make him feel better. With a posting-box he can! He can post a shape and make it be gone. But when he opens the lid, it is there again. He can take it out, make it go away, find it and post it again! He can control it to come and to go as *he* likes. It gives him the very important sense of 'I can do it!', 'I am someone!'

Linked with the concern over where oneself, and other things, go and belong, there is the desire to have things 'fit just so'. Will it fit nicely? Will it be a fit that gives him the snug comforting sense of 'just right'? Or will it jar and jam and feel uncomfortable? A shape that fits its designated hole beautifully must evoke deep memories of a satisfying feed, when the baby felt that the teat or nipple fitted just right, just what he had needed and wanted. Young children may see the hole of a posting-box, or indeed any hole, as some kind of gaping mouth that needs feeding or filling. This was my idea with Leila, who had found weaning very difficult and still demanded her bottle in her mouth all the time when she was four years old. With the posting-box discovery it became easier to wean her off her bottle. To everyone's surprise and relief Leila happily accepted a posting-box where in the past she would have demanded a bottle to stop her screaming.

Another familiar baby's 'posting' game in the wider sense, of 'in and out' and 'there and gone' is *his* feeding Mummy. It means the child understands that Mummy has a mouth and that he can put food into it:

> Fred did not seem to consider food offered to him at nursery to be eatable, and used it for some kind of messy play. But when his key-worker ate some of this food, making exaggerated noises of how much she was enjoying it, he looked up at her with interest. She held up some food on a fork to show him. He looked horrified, and then guided her hand firmly into her mouth as if saying 'You want that eaten? Then eat it yourself!' From then on Fred was interested in the food as something his key-worker could eat and spent many lunch-times feeding her – like a human posting-box for food stuff. Occasionally he also tasted a spoonful himself. Eventually, feeling that this game had become stuck, that he was ready to move on, his key-worker said to him firmly though casually '*You* eat it!' – and he did!

By being allowed to play with putting food into his key-worker, Fred was able to work through some of his anxieties about unfamiliar food. His key-worker's responsiveness encouraged him to develop a playful, less anxiety-driven attitude to the eating situation, which made the food feel safer for Fred. Needless to say, this 'eating game' also involved the all-important 'shared attention' and genuine eye contact.

Play with posting-boxes also helps with turn-taking. Initially we give him one shape at a time; later we actually take turns. It can easily be made to support speech and communication by naming the different shapes. Being aware of the far-ranging underlying principles means that the imaginative adult will be able to think of other creative ways of helping the autistic child develop the mental concepts and structures he needs for his cognitive, emotional, communicative and social development. The described principles can, for example, be transferred to tidying up, when this involves putting things into a toy-box with the adult pointing out each toy, or Lego-piece, that is to be picked up to help the child keep his mind on the task. Some children enjoy taking all the Lego out of its box themselves, not doing anything else with it: taking it all out – putting it all back in – that is the activity at this level of development. It is important for the adults to suppress their well-meaning impulse to tip the box out for him. Instead the game of Lego may need to be adapted into a game of 'In and Out', for example 'Let's take it all out – this one, and another one – and, look!, there are some more!'

... Well done! All out! – Now let's put them all back! This one, and that one, and another one, and ...' Although not very creative, such a cooperative purposeful activity of 'Lego out – Lego back in' is still an interactive activity.

If you can manage the jump to regarding tidying up, or emptying Lego out of its container as a very basic version of a posting-box, then you will agree that lots of things can be posted: almost anything that is around in the house, or nursery, can be made into the most simple pre-posting-box activity: he could post potatoes, onions, apples, lemons, corks, spoons, cups. The crucial principle in all this is that the container must be higher than it is wide (otherwise the disappearance trick does not work), so a cup, shallow container or open carton usually do not work. But a bucket, a clean waste-paper basket or a cardboard box that can be closed would do fine. A clean old oil-can, or other tall metal container, of course has the advantage that every cork, potato, spoon or shoe (why not!?) will make a satisfying clanking sound, as if acknowledging what it has received.

'He's Funny with Books!':
On Bridging the Gaps between Pages

Some autistic children show no interest in pictures or books at the age of four, others pick out books as a favourite choice, but then do not use them as intended. Being able to make sense of these flat two-dimensional things, i.e. pictures, as representations of the world is the result of complex processes of emotional and intellectual development. Pictures 'mean' something. Because of the autistic child's difficulty with 'meaning' he may be unable to make sense of pictures and what they depict, and just see patterns of colours and shapes.

> Adrian would stand in front of the book-rack as if studying the covers of the books, and adults were pleased about his interest in books. But when he picked a book, he put it into his mouth, excitedly running around. He liked the spines best. The corners too would soon end up with teeth marks, or chewed-off altogether. At first his teachers tried to show him pictures that might interest him. But Adrian simply ran away. Even if he *did* appear to be looking, no sense of recognition seemed to register on his face, as can be seen in someone's eyes and facial expressions. It seemed as if he simply did not know how to do it: how does one look at a picture so one sees what it is a picture of?

To Adrian, books were simply hard and square things that were nice to bite. It was probably not the covers or pictures he was looking at but the hardness, the 'bite-ability' of their spines. Anything hard could fulfil the function of Adrian's 'autistic object' (see chapter 7), and when the books were taken away, he did not mind and used other hard objects to bite on. Other autistic children seem to like looking at books, but then don't listen when they are read.

Cheng seemed to love books above anything else. As soon as he saw an adult sitting anywhere, he climbed on her lap with a book, opened it and the adult naturally began reading to him. But Cheng looked around the room, not at the pictures. Eventually, the adult would stop reading and talk to him about the pictures. But Cheng, his eyes still everywhere except on the book, showed no interest. If the adult began talking to another adult, Cheng did not mind – as long as she was talking.

Cheng seemed to have worked out that putting a book and an adult together would result in the adult creating a comfy seat with 'sound-system'. This is familiar to us from all young children who find it comforting to listen to the music of people talking. But something had gone dead about this for Cheng. He had come to expect that a book would get him a cosy place to sit, wrapped in sound. He was treating the adult like a better chair. But people are so much more than simply a warm seat. It was important to show Cheng that books are things to be read or looked at. But people are alive! People can listen and talk and play with him!

From then on, every time Cheng brought a book but stopped looking at the pictures, we would put the book away saying 'No book – byebye book: Cheng wants a cuddle!' or: 'Cheng wants to play!' (or whatever seemed appropriate). The adult would then engage him in an action song or an interactive game of the 'I'm gonna getcha!' kind. Within about a week, Cheng stopped bringing books to the adults. He still climbs onto their laps often, but without a book. Books are still important to him, and he now sometimes sits and looks at books – but unfortunately, he also takes his anger out on them, and bites and tears them.

Other autistic children do something else with books that puzzles people: they flick through every book, or one particular book only, at such speed that it is hard to believe they could be seeing anything. It has a similar automatic and controlling quality to flicking light-switches. It feels essentially meaningless, and mindless, making the adult want to rush over, with that same speed and urgency, shouting 'Stop that!'

I puzzled for months about what Terry was getting out of his flicking through books. Trying to talk to him about the pictures or to slow him down made him furious. He would insist, almost violently, on carrying on racing through the book, teeth clenched, his body tense, pinching and clawing at me in rage over my interference. He did not enjoy this activity at all. It looked like an awful ordeal. But it seemed impossible to relieve him and show him anything else. He seemed hooked on this painful activity, like an addiction, or a compulsion he was powerless against.

Was he pretending to read, perhaps like his older sister, but lacking the foundations of the meaning of pictures and words? We dismissed this idea as much too sophisticated for a child like Terry. All his other behaviour and responses showed that he had not yet mastered the earlier symbolic stages. Was he copying, just going through the motions, as if that were all there is to reading or looking at a book? Eventually, and after what felt like a very long time of watching without understanding anything (difficult to tolerate for anyone) it struck me that the very moment you turn the page, the previous page is 'gone'. If you find things being 'gone' difficult (which babies and young autistic children do), then you are in a quandary, because each page becomes a miniature anxiety attack, which makes it necessary to keep checking that everything is still 'there'! Hence Terry's distress, and the sense of him being mercilessly driven to check, check, check that none of the pages was gone! They may have run away, someone may have taken them away or changed them. Who knows? So he tried to look at them all at the same time, struggling as best as he could with the awkward invention of books. Why do they have to have pictures on both sides? While looking at one, the other one may fall off or disappear! All sorts of strange things have been known to occur in his short life in this strange world. So he watched them like a hawk, racing through the pages to keep up.

> The next time, I joined him by turning a page back and forth at his speed saying 'Don't like "gone"' and, turning back to the previous page 'There it is!', and back again saying 'Gone again!' and 'There again!', again and again. I 'echoed' his speed of leafing through the book, adding quick versions of the toddler preoccupation of 'Gone!' and 'There!'. He was clearly interested in this adapted version of peekaboo or hide-and-seek with the pages of a book. It had now become a game. We also played 'Where is it gone?' – 'There it is! ... Ooops, – gone again!'

His idea seemed to have been that if you go really quickly, you can almost see all the pictures in one look, one flash – and don't have to face the difficult idea of 'gone'. But although his method didn't work particularly well (or because books are in fact not particularly well-suited to this method), he insisted on trying to make his idea work. It was as if a book to Terry was more like a box or container, and he had to check that all its contents were still inside. But there is more to a picture-book than to a box of bricks. The contents of a book are usually held together not so much by its spine as by its story or topic. But these are mental concepts. The story, and the meaning of the pictures, need to be kept in mind, and it is the mind that has to become the container for the thoughts that are generated by the pictures of the story in a book. Terry found this very difficult. His mind would not hold such a complicated concept because he was still so preoccupied with gone-ness, a much earlier developmental stage. He needed help to find a different way of dealing with the problem of 'gone-ness' when it came to pictures and books. It seemed as if he was trying to traverse the ravines between pages without bridges. His mental model of treating them like a box or container with things inside really does not work well with books. He needed to be shown how to build bridges in his mind to connect the pages, so this dread of 'gone-ness' would not take him over with every page. Giving the experience names, calling it 'there' and 'gone' created such a bridge, and even allowed us to playfully cross it together.

With two copies of each picture of a book (perhaps mounted on a piece of card), one can insert one further, and more concrete, stage into this process: Terry could then line up all the pictures, thus enabling him to see them all at the same time, as well as comparing them with those in the book. There are other communicative games this allows for, like lotto games, picture-posting, picture-matching or 'Can you find this picture in the book?' The pictures could be put together to invent different stories, lined up 'wrongly' for him to sort into the correct order, and used during his day to make them personally significant for him, i.e. to encourage him to link pictures with meaning. We could, for example, show him a picture of a child eating a biscuit or going to the park, before giving him a biscuit, or going to the park.

When I met Terry again, about three years later, he had moved on from his racing through books, but had developed another odd way of dealing with them.

> He would insist that his teacher sat down to read a book to him, the same book every day. She read in a 'clipped' tone of voice, as he moved his finger from 'letter-bunch' to 'letter-bunch' (= words). This way he knew when the page needed turning.

Although his teacher was glad about Terry's interest in books, careful observation of his facial expression suggested that he was not in fact listening to the story or as she thought 'reading', borne out especially by his eyes, which often wandered around the room, while he continued to point to the 'letter-bunches'. He seemed to be *instructing* her to read, to make the correct noises for him to listen to. He seemed neither aware of the meaning of the story, nor to be interested in the letters that made up the different words. Again it felt as if he was doing something akin to flicking switches, in this case as if switching on his teacher's sound-making device. Something stale and potentially dead was going on here.

There was something quite bossy about Terry. His teacher did not particularly like it, but instead of saying so and offering Terry some more lively and creative opportunities, she simply 'suffered' his treatment. It seemed as if she had cut off herself, no longer cared whether it made sense or not, and just reacted, in an automatic fashion, like a sound machine, or one of those 'press-the-button' books. When I talked to her about Terry and his 'reading', she explained that she felt confused and did not understand what he was, or might be, doing, and what she should, or could, do to help him. She was also tired, fed up, bored and felt unsupported. It is possible that all these feelings were also communications from Terry about how *he* felt inside himself, which his teacher was quite sensitively picking up. With this information in mind, she may then have been able to think of ways to enliven both herself and Terry, to make their interactions more creative and lively in a human way and to communicate in ways that did not reduce her (or him) to some kind of automaton.

Our main aim is to keep things alive, and talking is one of the most alive and human ways of building bridges of human contact and interaction. It is crucial for us not to lose sight of humanity and hope, and to relate to and talk to the child *as if* he does have human potential for understanding. The child's blankness, although an autistic retreat, rarely obliterates all meaningful sound. At the same time we need to keep observing his smallest non-verbal communications with great care and respond accordingly. Books have great potential for all kinds of learning and enjoyment, but they can also be misused. The crucial importance of 'shared attention' for the later development of speech and language cannot be stressed often and strongly enough. And there can hardly be a more versatile tool to facilitate this than an adult and a child looking at a picture-book together.

PART III

TRYING TO MAKE SENSE OF IT

7
The Addictive Nature
of Autistic Behaviours

When a Cuddle is Not a Cuddle:
On Wanting to Be an 'Inside Baby'

Some young autistic children cry to be picked up and carried all the time, refusing any offers of other activities or games. The child clings to an adult – often any adult will do. It seems to be a cuddle, but somehow it isn't: he seems to get no comfort from it.

> Hanging limply in the adult's arms, his eyes trailing 'unseeingly' somewhere in the distance, Tim cried as soon as the adult tried to put him down, or even just sit down herself. The only way to stop the crying seemed to be picking him up – or walking out (in order not to hear it).

Young children need to be held and cuddled, and most adults are only too happy to pick up a young child stretching up his arms. He may have got scared, feel lost or alone, tired or bored. He comes to recharge his emotional resources, to remind himself that he belongs to someone, to take a rest in a secure place. Having 'refuelled' he is ready to get on with exploring, playing and learning. But although clingy, and perhaps shy, these children watch what is going on around them from the safety of the adult's arm, actively trying to get the adult's attention and to engage in little interactive games with looks, smiles and vocal sounds.

The cuddles with the autistic child are so different, and difficult, because all this is missing. All he wants to do, is sit. Nothing more. Just sitting, often with his eyes closed or vacant. He does not want to find out and explore. He seems to want time to stand still. He is not interested in growth and development, because that spells change – and he is against change. He wants everything to stay the same. But wanting to keep everything the same, to stop things from developing naturally, is the greatest obstacle to mental growth. It has the 'anti-developmental' quality of an addiction. And the child's unresponsiveness paired with his adamant insistence on being passively needy, sometimes in a limp and apparently helpless way, together with getting the adult to make all the effort, is very difficult to deal with.

If we as adults dare to monitor our feelings, we may be horrified. We feel for the child, we so much want to help him. But somehow one feels subtly coerced, without being properly aware of it, into doing something awful. There is something going on that one hates, that makes us feel so bad. But all this poor darling wants is a cuddle. How could we refuse? Adults often get into an emotional muddle as to how to respond. On the one hand we want to push him away because the way this cuddle is being asked for, and how it is used feels horrible – on the other, we then feel guilty because he is only little and obviously he needs a cuddle, and we don't want to feel we are being cruel.

> All Kofi wanted to do was sit on the lap of an adult, who often wondered how Kofi had got there – she could not remember picking him up. Burying his face into her, he shut off and withdrew, screaming furiously every time the adult moved or spoke, as if demanding: 'Just sit and be still!'

Neither Kofi nor Tim looked around or followed anything with their eyes. They had no interest in interaction, fiercely warding off any approaches.

The autistic child gives himself over completely to some sensations, almost blindly and as if he could not hear. All his attention seems to be absorbed by the sensation of his skin, of being held, stroked and cuddled. It is as if he had switched off all other sensory channels, as if 'bathing' in that close skin sensation, reminding him of what life had felt like before he was born: still at one with his mummy, in her tummy. He seems to want to merge with the adult as if they were not two people but only one. If he keeps totally still, nothing seems to contradict this illusion, and he can be oblivious of their separateness – until the adult moves, or talks! At that moment Kofi lashes out with furious screaming at the adult who has just shattered his dream. We may know the state of mind Kofi is trying to create from the half-consciousness we all know just before actually falling asleep or waking up properly: a blissful state of relaxation, almost as if dissolving in those peaceful, lovely sensations. The big difference is that Kofi insists on being in this state *all* the time, all *day* long – and not only as a momentary transition into the unconscious realms of sleep.

The state Kofi and Tim are trying to recreate I call 'wanting to be an "inside baby"': as if not yet born, still one with his mummy and the rest of the world. Before he was born he did not have to bother with looking and listening, with responding and playing. He could feel something firm and soft all around him, giving him a sense of comforting containment. Sounds were muffled and not as sharp as when people are speaking nowadays. Out here he feels raw, exposed and frightened, so much so that he tries with all his might to force his way back to the time when he felt safe as an 'inside baby'. To such children 'outside' is 'adrift in space without a space-suit' (Bick 1968). He's tried it out here. He doesn't think much of it, and concludes: 'I'm going back!'

While in a pure sensation-state of being an 'inside baby', the child will be content. But all his attention is absorbed away from focussing on any mental, interactive, communicative or cognitive activity. We can see this in how angrily Kofi rejects offers of tickling and face-to-face games from the adult (or how irritated *we* become if a fly keeps buzzing past, or someone keeps calling our name when we are just about to drift off into sleep). Both Kofi and Tim seemed to make an actual effort not to engage in any social games, which means making an effort *not* to learn anything, i.e. *not* to allow any stimulation from social play and interaction to develop new connections between nerve cells in their brain: a truly anti- developmental effort to their own greatest disadvantage.

Our big problem is: how do we get across to the autistic child that going back is, unfortunately, not possible – that being alive and separate, that being an 'outside baby' isn't such a bad thing after all. In fact, it can be interesting and enjoyable in many different ways: there are the joys of learning, choosing, eating, playing, talking and so many others to compensate for what has been lost. Of course an 'inside baby' will feel vulnerable, when he suddenly finds himself in the outside world. If we want to convert a convinced 'inside baby', such as Kofi or Tim, to the life of an 'outside baby', we need to go about it slowly and gently, but at the same time firmly and reliably. He will not learn this simply by being pushed away every time he demands to be picked up – nor by giving in to his demands.

Some adults get great comfort themselves from holding a small, cuddly child in their arms. They may feel needy themselves, craving hugs and physical contact. Holding on to a child may be such a relief that they forget to think about the child's developmental needs, and whether, and how much of this is good for him. Picking him up, cuddling him, holding him, letting him cling to you: are you doing it for your own benefit, or for his? Be honest. Although Kofi was no doubt dearly loved, he was carried and cuddled, irrespective of his needs or wishes, because his family enjoyed it for themselves. To them he was at times more like a soft teddy bear than a small person needing space for himself to become independent.

It was different in Tim's case. While pregnant with him, his mother learnt that she had a serious illness which left her feeling exhausted. In order not to affect the baby, it could only be treated with drugs several months after

Tim's birth. A mother like Tim's may have had times of being preoccupied, of being lost in her own world of worries, perhaps even moments of deep and paralysing depression. The best she could do was to hold on to the child. During such times the baby may have become used to being someone else's teddy, comforter or pet. He may have come to feel that the adult wants and needs him to be this way. Both mother and child may have got used to merging with each other, and may have found it equally painful to separate and let go of the other.

What is so crucially missing is nothing more than the little bit of distance and 'in between space' that is necessary to play mouth and face games. It is not possible to communicate or interact with someone if you are so close as to be stuck on like a plaster on a sore place, touching the book with your eyes or hugging it to your chest. We need a little distance to look at someone's face, to reach out for things that catch our interest, to learn to copy and talk. A convinced 'inside baby' needs us to help him create, and to learn to tolerate, some 'in between space', between himself and the other person. He needs us to show him that being an 'outside baby' does not have to feel like being lost in space without a space-suit – which would indeed be terribly scary. He needs to feel that an adult's lively mind is on him with firm attention, watching his tiniest responses and signs of what he is feeling, especially in his face.

We want to discourage his clinging. But at the same time we want to encourage his awareness that we can be in contact even without touching. We know that it is perfectly possible to be in touch with another person *mentally* without touching skin to skin. But does *he* know? We can try to show him with our eyes, our face, our voice. We can call on his attention with some urgency. We can do so by describing to him what he is doing, what he seems to be feeling, what is going on around him. We can also make a special effort to resist cuddling, touching, tickling and hugging him too much, encouraging physical separateness and his sense of independence. While he likes nice sensations, we want to help him to connect these with more mental cognitive awareness, i.e. only touching him *when it 'tugs' at his mental capacities*, for instance an 'I'm gonna getcha!' game can culminate in 'I'm gonna *touch* your nose!', rather than a tickle. Hiding games, peekaboo and 'I'm gonna getcha!' games play with just this issue, and so do mouth and face and all face-to-face baby games.

It is the adult's firm and attentive mind that provides the 'space-suit' for any newborn baby and for the reluctant beginner 'outside baby' such as Kofi or Tim. It is hard work for the adult. To provide the child with a firm sense of containment demands from us a very great deal of constant effort and attention, unselfishness and self-discipline, awareness and sensitivity, mindfulness and concentration.

When a Toy is Neither a Toy Nor a Comforter: What Is an 'Autistic Object' Good For?

Many autistic children insist on constantly clutching some toy or object. Anything will do – a small car, a wooden brick, an action-man, a bunch of keys, *any* bunch of keys. They never play with it. It's only purpose seems to be *having* it. Try taking it away, and you are asking for trouble. Big, massive trouble of the ear-piercing screams and tantrum variety! Give it back and there'll be peace again. Without a doubt, this toy or object fulfils some vital function for the child. But there is something about it that gets adults all frazzled and worried. If it was like the teddy bear, soft cuddly toy or security blanket which some children need for some time, we could understand his need for such a comforter, knowing that he will grow out of it. But the autistic child's clinging has a very different feel. Adults often feel compelled to take it away, with his best interests in mind. Whether that is the right thing or not, they are never sure.

The moment Adrian arrived at the nursery, he picked up some object, any hard object, which he would then hang on to for the rest of the day, often holding it with his teeth. Initially it was a bright green toy basket. But if the 'green thing' was taken away, he would simply pick up something else to bite on. He liked books for their hard spine and corners, or wooden puzzle pieces. Soon all these disappeared (put away because his biting was wrecking them). None of these objects he used, or played with, as they were intended. With the object in his mouth, his eyes seemed to 'switch off', and usually he would also be running up and down.

Watching Adrian closely and over time, it seemed as if he chose objects according to certain criteria of 'bite-ability'and shape, like sharp corners, holes and something like a handle. A large wooden puzzle-piece has something like a 'handle' to hold it by and so did the 'green thing'. Another of his favourites was a plastic toy frying pan, inset-tray pieces with knobs or any toy with something sticking out to hold it by, and – Adrian being Adrian – he 'held' them not with his hands but with his teeth.

Fred was inseparable from his little car. Any small car would do. But a car it had to be. If the one he was holding was taken away, he just picked up another one. Occasionally he would fight like a lion to keep or get a particular car. He would carry it pressed into his hand, or lie with his head on the floor pushing it up and down. Careful observation of his eye movements showed that he was not actually playing: he was watching its wheels go round. Sometimes he sat turning the wheels with his fingers. He could easily do this for what seemed to be forever!

Typically, the adult's instinctive response is one of helpless irritation – partly in response to one's hurt over feeling so wilfuly ignored. The urge to simply want to take 'that thing' away is fuelled by an underlying sense that what the autistic child is doing with it has no developmental value – it actually prevents him from learning anything. But taking it away is seldom successful: the child usually gets so upset that his toy is soon returned to him. Or he simply picks up any other hard toy to cling to with the same tenacity. We may need to accept that it might not be possible to stop him like this – and that we may, in fact, be creating worse scenarios.

These children's objects share certain common characteristics: hard with sharp corners, often with holes, and often with bits sticking out that can be fiddled with, for instance switches or wheels that can be spun. Usually replaceable by any other hard object, it is often held so tightly in the hand that it leaves an imprint in his skin. It has no imaginative qualities and is not played with in creative or symbolic ways. If it is a book, it is favoured for its hardness and squareness, not its pictures. Any attempt to take away his 'autistic object' (Tustin 1981) is met with fierce screaming, an earth-shattering tantrum or aggression not seen in this particular child at any other time.

The difference between an autistic object and another child's teddy, comforter or other 'transitional object' (like Linus' blanket in the cartoon *Peanuts*) is that the autistic child's clinging actively *excludes* any other person. A child needing his teddy or special blanket clutches it to help him cope with the world. In contrast, the autistic child's clinging to his hard object is an entirely solitary activity, designed to shut out awareness of anything going on around him. With the autistic child the natural exploratory drives of the young baby or toddler, so important for healthy development, have become stuck, like wheels in thick mud going round and round without progress or forward movement. He does not want to know about going anywhere, not about development, not about change. His main concern seems to be to create a 'me world' like that of the 'inside baby' who does not yet have to tackle the challenges of the outside 'not-me' world.

The persistent clinging, and the fact that it is never played with in any imaginative, or even functional, way suggests that the autistic child's object (or the sensation it creates on his skin) is not experienced as a separate object, but as a part of himself, like the turtle's shell, the hedgehog's spikes, the snail's house. Take off the turtle's shell, the hedgehog's spikes, the snail's house, and you have an utterly defenceless bit of an animal – or one more dead than alive. The autistic child's experience is fraught with terror: fears as if his body did not belong to him, that bits of his body might fall off, of being swallowed up by a 'black hole', of dissolving, leaking, melting, falling to bits or disintegrating like a sandcastle when the tide draws in, or a Lego structure dropped on the floor. So much of his awareness, so much of his mind has already slipped away! He feels so small, so insubstantial, so insecure. Is he really there? Does he really exist? He is not sure, not sure at all. And with this he quickly grabs hold of anything hard and solid, a car, an action-man – any hard plastic toy. But while clinging to his autistic object is meant to protect him from anything different or frightening, in fact it only increases his terror of change and separation. It makes exploration a torture and, worst of all, offers no real protection at all. Just think how easily it is snatched away by an adult!

The autistic child tries to deal with his fears all by himself, to be totally self-sufficient, not needing anybody. He seeks his comfort in bodily sensations, which he controls, rather than from unpredictable human contact, or a real mothering person. Feeling the object's hard edges in his hand or against his teeth, feeling the comforting rhythm of his repetitive twiddling, confirms his sense of the solidity of his body inside his skin – because it gives him the sensation of something solid, ongoing and sub-stantial. The object's solidness makes him feel more solid and strong himself, when inside he is actually feeling so soft and frightened and vulnerable. To him, his 'autistic object' is like a talisman with magical powers, vital for survival. Strengthened by his autistic object he feels like one hard 'autistic-object child' that is so solid that nothing can hurt or frighten him. As far as he is concerned, he's got it all sorted. The rest of the world can go to hell: nothing in it for him. But then someone, or something, from the outside world pierces his 'me-world cocoon' and exposes it as the illusion it is. That's when there is going to be a furious tantrum, or a desperate grab for another hard object.

The trouble is that the autistic child uses his hard object like a bath-plug to shut off, or plug up, his mind, leaving no channels of awareness, attention or interest. Often his eyes and face go vacant while clutching or biting it. He cocoons himself in his 'me world', and uses some hard object or repetitive activity to fill it with thrills and excitement, such as excited flapping or spinning, jumping or running. This can quickly become a persistent habit, which he is driven to indulge in repetitively and compul-sively, without meaning, because he does not know any other ways of how to be and what to do. Because all his energy and attention is focussed on the sensation (tactile via his teeth with Adrian, visual with the wheels of Fred's car), there is none left to attend to anything else. The autistic object not only plugs up any anxious feeling. It also plugs up all his awareness of the outside world.

It is this anti-developmental aspect of cutting off that adults intuitively want to stop by taking the object away. They want to free his mind for more active exploration, awareness of his environment, without which no learning is possible. Unlike a toy, the autistic object seems to be a hindrance to doing anything at all, tying up at least one of his hands, or his mouth, for holding it and, what is worse, all his attention with none left to attend to anything else, so he seems not to hear, see or be aware of anything. The adults' intuition is of course correct: the autistic object does indeed inhibit all development (mental, cognitive, emotional, even physical) by tying up any available energy and curiosity. The total absorption with his autistic object blocks his ability to learn and to engage with the world around and with other people. This is the point where we have to position our efforts. How can we entice him to come out of his cocoon – show him that the outside world, that 'not-me' world so dreaded by him, can be fun and worthwhile?

Being aware of his anxieties helps us to be sensitive to the autistic child's fearful, perhaps even terrified feelings. Simply taking the object away may feel to him like losing the comforting sensation of solidness he needs it for, and with that his own sense of continuity and self. His screaming may be like his contents spilling out of the hole, which he feels has been torn into his body-self when his autistic object is yanked away like sugar out of a tear in the bag. Before this habit can develop its own momentum (usually not under the age of three), we want to find playful ways to coax him out into our shared world of human interaction, using a gentle and thoughtful approach, applied with warmth as well as firmness and discipline, without wrenching out what he may feel is part of himself.

Our aim is to draw him into simple interactive fun games, which either include the autistic object or ignore it. Sometimes this can be just talking about what he is doing, pointing out what is going on around him, or what else he could do with his toy. It is often possible to integrate his object into a simple interactive game, like the most basic baby turn-taking game of taking and giving it back instantaneously. Perhaps he can be encouraged to roll his car in 'ready–steady —— go!' fashion as far as it will go, or to and fro with his key-worker.

> Fred's key-worker finally managed to catch and hold Fred's attention by creating suspenseful anticipation he could not resist with simple 'ready–steady–go' patterns and to win him into shared enjoyment of using his car to play with her.

Some children will join in pre-turn-taking activities of being offered a different toy and another and another, so the activity in fact becomes an interactive game of you giving and him taking things from you, for example offering him a box full of his favourite objects. In this way he practises at least letting go of his object, focussing his attention in order to look and choose something else – all in response to another person's communicative approaches. This also gives the adult the opportunity to talk to him a little, with more chances of reaching him during those more focussed moments.

Whenever we do have to take away his autistic object, we need to prepare him by talking to him about it first. One cannot eat or get dressed or hold hands for a circle song with a toy in one's hand or mouth. But it does not need to be the wrenching-out or yanking-away approach. Because of the importance the autistic object has for him, we need to give him plenty of warning if we expect him to give it up. We need to tell him – and wait, giving him time to respond with dignity:

> 'Fred, it is time for songs. You need to put your car away now.' Fred may run away in defiance, or appear not to hear. His key-worker, waiting expectantly, repeats: 'Can I have it now, please?', stretching out her hand patiently but firmly. As with a much younger toddler, she may begin to sing one of the familiar songs holding his hands securely and looking at him with encouraging attentive eyes, while putting away his car in a matter-of-fact way. If he feels securely held by her full attentiveness on him, he will be more able to let go of his toy and his insecurity.
>
> Adrian was not reachable with words like this. But several verbal warnings at least prepared him that 'something was up'. The adult would say 'Adrian, it is dinner-time now. I will take "it" away now', perhaps three times, before actually doing so.

We need to help him to make a transition without unleashing such a storm of panic or rage that he is again unable to attend to what is going on. Sometimes putting the car into his pocket helps, because he can still feel it on his skin. Sometimes we cannot prevent him getting upset. But we must make sure that we help him move into the new activity without interrupting his sense of continuity. The clinging persists because of fear. It can become a terribly self-destructive habit, so our aims must be to introduce some fun, humour and human interaction into his solitary activities, or to find ways to endow the autistic object with emotional meaning by giving it a function that is shared between both of us.

'Why Is He Jigging Something All the Time?': The Hypnotic Power of Anything

While many autistic children appear to need the sensation of a hard toy or object, others use the bodily sensations of rhythmic movement to make them feel safe. They wave, shake, swing, spin, suck, bite, bounce, jig, click, flick, flip or flap something, usually in a fast, perhaps even frenzied, rhythm and often running around too. Others create the same effect of bodily sensations by rocking, jumping, clapping, blinking, stroking, hand-flapping, tongue-wiggling, head-banging, hand-biting, and so on.

> Derek developed a taste for 'jigging' things after his nursery once hung up a bouncy ball on an elastic. He loved it, in fact he seemed to get 'high' on it, and seemed to have become addicted to the rhythmic movement of anything that could be 'jigged' or dangled, including telephones, dolls and books which can be jigged by their hair or pages. If prevented from this, he simply created the same rhythmic sensation by wiggling his tongue in his mouth.
>
> When Gary was stopped from continuously tossing his small red ball, he would flap his hands instead. Holding them very loosely so they flopped down from his wrists, he 'jigged' them just as Derek did with stringed objects, transfixed by the movement, staring with rapt attention as if 'in seventh heaven'.

While engaged in the various repetitive activities, the autistic child seems completely absorbed, even thrilled, a glazed look in his eyes, apparently blind to anything else around him. Nothing can distract him. It looks as if he would carry on with this for ever and ever, as if he had found a secret and wonderful place, which no one could ever take him away from.

What all these activities have in common is a rhythmic movement that is endlessly repeated and entirely under his control. Their aim seems to be to create a predictable and familiar situation that will go on and always stay the same. The autistic child's excitement is generated by the *hypnotic power* the rhythm has which is made to pulse through his body. This ongoing sensory stimulation envelops him in such a way that it absorbs all of his attention and awareness to the exclusion of all else. It envelops him in a sense of rhythmic sensation that has the same function as that provided by the hard, solid sensation of the 'autistic object', or that of wanting to be an 'inside baby'. Wanting to avoid all awareness of the unpredictable outside world, he becomes instead engrossed in some physical sensation, with the simultaneous draining away of his mind. Instead of being overwhelmed by feelings of insecurity, he diverts his attention and focusses it firmly onto the sensation of the car pressed into his hand, the tapping of some hard toy against his teeth, the rhythm of his jigging, the sensation of dangling or flapping, or water running on and on from the tap in a never-ending stream.

Its real purpose we can perhaps see when we try to stop it, and the child seems overrun with unbearable panic or tantrum, as if beside himself with rage or on the edge of an abyss. Often his screaming or crying only stops when he is allowed to continue his rhythmic activity of rocking, jigging, flapping, with what appears to be a self-soothing function of plugging up some awful black hole of panic and inner chaos. Derek's 'jigging', as we later found out, also coincided with the time when his father had begun to threaten the four-year-old with a stick, in a desperate attempt to make this very insecure little boy into a 'real boy'. After this Derek gave up all interest in human interaction, from which he had derived some enjoyment before.

When 'hypnotised' in this way, the child tends not only to be oblivious of anything going on around him. He will also resist any interference, for example suggestions of other activities, with all his might. But while engaged in this hypnotising activity he is essentially in a mindless state. It is this that so upsets his carers, their instinctive gut-reaction being that this is not in the service of his psychological growth. Its main purpose seems to be to simply make time pass. While enveloping himself in his self-soothing rhythmic sensations, his cognitive, mental or intellectual brain activity seems at a standstill – with only the screensaver on.

Knowing that the attraction lies in his obsessional interest in rhythmic movement allows us to think of ways to counteract its hypnotic power – or to make it interactive. The toy that is used in an obsessive and mindlessly repetitive way can be used for simple interactive activities that are based on rhythm, but in a more human and alive way – such as playfully and gently teasing turn-taking games (see chapters 4 and 6). There is clearly something the child seems to need. But leaving him in his lonely world of rhythm, that is essentially so empty, will not help him develop other ideas for dealing with the world. We want to introduce, drip by drip, something more alive and human, something more social and interactive, more ordinary and communicative into his solitary stuckness. We can echo his rhythm in all sorts of ways, adding to his body sensations, for example by tapping it on his arm or shoulder, rubbing his back or leg in his rhythm, even taking another toy and jigging it just like him and together. We can speak, sing, grunt, make funny faces and silly noises, we can even wiggle our tongue all in the same repetitive rhythm as his jigging.

He will be surprised to see his rhythm repeated out there! And this surprise is wonderful, because it means he will throw us a brief puzzled glance. His sense had been that this rhythm was just *him*. So how come it is suddenly both inside him *and* outside? A moment of curiosity, a tiny bit of mental space has got in between his jigging, flapping, wiggling, which attracts more of his attention, if only momentarily. Trying to 'get in' on what the child is doing without actively interfering too much is generally successful. Sometimes it might just be sitting nearby and describing what he is doing, giving some kind of running commentary (see chapter 2). Or we can try to join in a little more actively, trying to expand, widen and stretch his activity – as long as we can be sure of being very clearly playful and flexible, willing to pull back immediately after even a tiny advance, should we notice signs of fearfulness in his body language. Fatima used to spend much of the day running around the room banging together two identical objects – wooden bricks, dolls' hairbrushes, cups, and so on.

Eventually Fatima allowed me to have a go at clapping together her two objects, when I begged 'Can I have a go? Please???', then copying her exactly before handing them back immediately. Sometimes she held them between thumb and index finger, sometimes between thumb and little finger, sometimes firmly, sometimes loosely. The rhythms also changed. I would talk to her like a much younger child: '"Tap-tap-tap!' – Oh Fatima is holding them *that* way! "Tap-tap-tap!"' After about two weeks she offered them to me voluntarily to have my turn, as she was sure that I would hand them back again instantly, and it was fun. That was our little game, our little conversation. Only a few seconds at a time – but a spontaneous turn-taking communication it was!

Sometimes children can get very over-excited while 'hypnotised' by their rhythms. The child who has got himself into a giggling mode (that sometimes makes adults even wonder secretly if he is mad), may truly have got lost in a state that is light-years away from where we are. He may indeed be unable to find the way out of some kind of trance-like state and back into the ordinary world of human beings and communication. Calling on his humanity with 'Hey, come back now!', said in a light enough tone of voice that is playful, welcoming and not hot-and-bothered, just wanting to inform him that 'Hey! You are in a place I'm not in – and you are welcome to come and join me!' is sometimes enough to get through to him in his faraway place. At other times a more urgent tone of voice is required to express our alarm, lest he gets himself too comfortable in a state, or place, which is so far away that no one will be able to reach him.

When Clive is in such a far-away space, I call him with some playful urgency: 'Hello!?', not unlike calling at someone's locked door to see whether they aren't in after all. This almost always gets him to 'come back', answering 'hello' in turn, looking at me as if I had brought him up from somewhere deep down. Sometimes I add a smiling 'Where are you??', as if calling for a child hiding nearby. Then he looks up and anwers a grinning 'Here I am!', as if delighted at having been found.

As with a much younger child, we also need to remember that we can add imaginative ideas and suggestions he would never have thought of by himself. Mothers do this naturally with their young babies. Many autistic children have so much to catch up with from their developmental arrest, that we do not want to leave any opportunity unused to help them. At the very least we want to show them the pleasure and safety of *having* ideas and imagination, lending our imagination to someone who has little or none. We never know what he may be able to use or learn.

With Derek one could add the briefest 'Oh, I think this could be an aeroplane! – Shhh – flies the plane! Derek's plane is flying in the air!' while using his toy without taking it out of his hand. Or we may think of 'Are you fishing? I think you may have caught a fish here. There is the fish! Yum yum, fish. Oops, gone again! – My hands can swim like a fish too! ...[singing] 1 – 2 – 3, 4, 5, once I caught a fish alive ...'

Any fun idea that comes to our mind will do to enliven his repetitive 'game', which isn't really a game at all, but more a way of whiling away time. It does not matter whether he really understands what we are talking about, as long as we manage to have fun together.

8
Focussing on Body Sensations without Meaning

Letting the Mind Fall Apart: About Seeing, Sensations and Not Making Sense

While some autistic children are very active, others want to lie passively in a corner all day. Initially people think 'Oh, he is just tired today.' But his eyes are open. So they hope that 'he is watching'. But nothing catches his attention, which begins to raise doubts as to whether he really is watching. Trying to involve him in any activity also tends to prove fruitless. Tim would just let himself sag like a sack of potatoes, Kofi would scream as if he were being murdered, Adrian would chuckle and simply slip away. All would soon end up in some corner again, a vacant expression on their faces, doing nothing. What is happening to their attention?

We are not usually aware of all the things one can 'do' with one's mind and attention, especially the possiblity of disconnecting our mind and our perceptual organs, particularly the eyes: one can look at something but keep one's mind, attention and thinking switched off, or connect it differently, for example to what one is hearing or feeling on one's skin. There are all sorts of ways of seeing and using one's eyes. We all use them without being aware of it, but some autistic children may use all or some of them some or all of the time. Their looking often has a quality of engaging superficially without properly coming into gear – like a car on a foggy morning, noisy without going anywhere, or a computer failing to boot up. Some look 'through' people as if they were transparent, watch from the corner of their eye, or use their eyes to create a sensation of merging with the other person. To others seeing seems to be an almost tactile experience of 'stroking' what they see with their eyes without mentally taking it in.

Although Adrian apparently made such good eye contact, he actually seemed to 'lock' his eyes into the other person's in a way that made his looking feel like a solid rod. It seemed to fix our connection as if he could make it so solid that he could 'merge into me' through my eyes, creating a nice 'Adrian–me feeling'. There was no sense of there being two separate people – although it was not quite clear which one of us was gone, Adrian or me.

At other times his eye movements and general responses gave an impression as if, instead of really looking (which is an active process), he would 'rest' his eyes on what he was looking at, that someone's face would become a resting-place for his eyes, just as we may 'rest our eyes' on a beautiful landscape, and the face of someone speaking to him may be to Adrian what sheep moving about in the distant fields are to someone else.

While trying to understand and imagine what may be going on in the autistic child's mind in his apparently attentionless states, I observed myself being able to slip into a mode of seeing that seemed to have many of the observed hallmarks, when left to wait in an office by myself one day, feeling vaguely bored and passive. Letting my eyes stray absentmindedly out of the sixteenth-floor window onto the unfamiliar scene below, I suddenly became aware of the nature of my experience at that moment:

... a long red-white-blue thing passes from left to right through my field of vision, is gone, then from right to left. It means nothing. Just colourful beads in a soothing rhythm. If I switch off all my awareness of time, I can 'become' the red-white-blue movement, merge with it, be it.

When the person I had been waiting for entered, and intruded on my 'cloud nine' of timelessness, I was aware of a sense of reluctance, and reminded of the autistic children who often respond so reluctantly to our calls for interaction. Having to leave this timeless careless red-white-blue bliss-bubble in order to attend to the human complexities was disagreeable!

I was surprised to find that it was possible to look and see without engaging emotionally, to 'switch off' the meaning of what I saw, deliberately or simply letting it slip away by not keeping my 'mental grip' on it: I had been gazing at the comings and goings of London's Docklands Light Railway trains like patterns with no more significance than the water of the fountain in the courtyard below, resting my eyes on the movement – nothing other than a visual sensual experience with a surface quality without any emotional depth. Nice colours perhaps. It was perception as sensation, rather than perception as cognitive activity that is linked with cognitive processes of generating meaning.

In this mode of perception, what is seen, heard and noticed is either devoid of any of its potential meaning, which would be tied together by ideas, memories or associations that could be shared with and communicated to another person – or it is stripped of it. I can watch the train coming and going from my high window and wonder about it, for example where it is going, liking its colours, planning to travel on it. But it is also possible to disconnect one's thoughts from the simple act of seeing so it has no meaning or significance, just watching 'it' go past (whatever 'it' is), waiting blankly for whatever might be next ... coming-gone, coming-gone ... endlessly and without thinking or emotional engagement. No questions asked, no thoughts, no fantasies, no desire other than for that nice soft feeling-state of non-involvement to continue. The process in which someone's mind is stripped of its meaning-giving qualities is sometimes referred to as 'dismantling' (Meltzer 1975), which can be a passive process that happens inadvertently, as if by itself, or a more active, deliberate one.

This mental absorption in (usually moving) patterns can be applied to any context, for example becoming absorbed in the movement of the leaves of a tree, feeling one was being rocked lightly, or watching moving clouds, feeling oneself carefree and leisurely drifting along. It could be described as *two-dimensional perception* that is only attentive to the surface perception, to patterns of movement or colour or texture with emphasis on a sense of ongoingness (Williams 1996). The same principle of disengaged perception can then also be applied to the to and fro of others in the nursery, around the dinner table, of dishes being passed, put down, moved, of spoons being lifted and lowered, lifted and lowered. It is relatively easy to do with TV, where you can let the movement from the screen and the sounds wash over you without attending to what it is about, or that it is about anything at all – just a method of timeless time passing timelessly ... or a mindless 'dismantled' state, with very little mental activity going on.

Some autistic children seem to have got into a habit of simply, and passively, letting their mind and mental activity slip away. Others seem at times genuinely unable to stop their senses from falling apart, to make the mental link between what they hear and see. Some can't get a mental 'grip' on it and eagerly make use of an adult's offer to try to pull things together *for* them. Others seem to relish this state of weightless 'mindlessness', apparently making an actual effort, in much more deliberate ways, to keep their mind and their own capacity for multi-sensory perception in a dismantled state. Nobody knows for sure how and why they do this, or why it happens. What is certain is that they do not know how else to do it, or how *not* to do it. They need our help to learn, or relearn, that there are other ways of using one's mind than those to which they have become used, or addicted.

What allowed me the choice to remain in or to emerge from my absent-minded state of pattern-gazing, was my ability to observe myself and to think about what I was observing. The ability to think about things is closely linked with language, with being able to name and put words to our experience. This is what can get us out of such states, and it shows again the importance of talking and giving a name to the experiences and feelings the autistic child is or may be having. If he can connect a certain state with a shared word or name, he may be able to catch himself having this experience, and with much practice and help he may even become able to stop or change it.

I find it helpful to think of those small, old-fashioned toy animals made from beads and held up by string on a hollow base: if pushed in with one's thumb the string connections loosen and the animal wiggles its ears, nods its head, eats, dances, wags, or droops tail and ears. If pressed in completely, or if the string is broken, the little animal collapses into a heap of beads. The autistic child sometimes seems as if his 'string connections' have come loose and he has collapsed into a small heap of apparently unconnected bits of perceptions – his hearing in one corner of the room, his seeing in another, his attention gone or turned inwards on skin sensations. But with sensitive observation and patience trying out what might 'get him', some connect-edness can usually be established:

Tim used to insist, in a passive sort of way, on lounging around in some corner, his mind apparently switched off or fallen apart, his eyes arrested in an unseeing far-away position. But by making an enormous, and at the same time very low-key and casual-seeming effort to attract his attention with the most interesting noises I could think to make with my mouth (mouth and face games), it was possible to get him to make communicative eye contact for several minutes.

It is interesting to see how enough of an adult's sensitively persistent, though low-key and admittedly gigantic, efforts could produce some change in Tim's state of mind, which otherwise seemed to be flaccid as he let it slip away like a snake disappearing in wet grass. But if one chased after him (mentally, I mean), one could find him again. The force of this three-year-old's insistence on averting his eyes, on not engaging (although he could), on letting his mind go blank, always seemed like a huge contradiction to his passivity. He seemed to have much more mental effort and energy available than he was letting on, or knew how to use. His insistence had to find its match in sensitive but equally persistent adult efforts to help him 'reclaim' his own lost mind connections.

> Patrick, always busy with some activity, often seemed invisible. He never asked for attention, never for a cuddle, and only rarely for help. Other people didn't bother him, they simply seemed not to exist. At the end of the day, I often realised that, despite repeated efforts to spend time with him, he had again slipped out of my mind like too small a fish through a net.

This in itself was a communication from Patrick, a message about himself he had placed into me, i.e.: 'links and connections slip from one's mind and it is very difficult to hold on to and make a resilient-enough link with another person'. As with Tim, one had to make a great effort to get Patrick's attention. While Tim stayed in one place, his mind apparently lost or fallen apart, Patrick one had to follow around in order to stay in touch with him, and to interrupt his solitary pursuits, actively inviting him into interactive ones. Then he would join in with delight, even adding his own suggestions into our developing game, laughing and suddenly making good eye contact (see chapter 5). A week later he came frequently to 'ask' for repeats of our new game, and it seemed as if he was beginning to develop an expectation of non-slip minds, his and mine.

We all know that a real relationship with a sensitively attuned person is crucial for the physical as well as mental well-being of every baby. The motivation to connect up one's senses seems to grow only in a safe human relationship, with the connection of the relationship to connect up the senses. The world feels connected and begins to make sense to the child, because he feels connected in his relationship with his mum (or other significant carer), and he begins to be able to (re-)connect his senses, to feel that the world makes sense and to be able to make sense of the world in turn. Feeling emotionally connected is fundamental to the development of meaning and things making sense, because it stirs a sense of curiosity and focusses attention.

By attracting and holding his attention with our own mental focussing (mainly expressed in our facial expressions), it is possible to help the autistic child to pull together some of his own mental functions. In doing this, we are providing him with a model of focussed concentration which he can watch, take in and copy. By actively helping him to pull and hold together his different senses of eyes, ears, touch, smell and others, we help him to 'mentalise' his experience. With some understanding of the underlying mental mechanisms at work it is sometimes possible to tighten the inter-sensory connections and to entice the autistic child out of his uni-sensory mode into at least a 'dual carriageway' of perception. In pulling together his different senses into attentiveness, 'unseeing seeing' can become curious looking, and detached hearing can become interested listening. Close observation of very young babies also shows that the ability to make sense of what they hear, see, and experience needs the presence of another familiar person as the 'central cohesive force' (Frith 1989) to help the infant draw together and connect up his senses. It is such 'live company' (Alvarez 1992), and our active and sensitive attention, that is needed to help the autistic child to reconnect with more mentally active modes of experience.

Lost in Skin and Bodily Sensations: Sensation Minus Meaning

Autistic children have fundamental difficulties with meaning, feelings and emotion. So what is going on when the autistic child is passively lying around, relentlessly running up and down or absorbed in his puzzling behaviours? If we substract meaning and emotional feeling from our experience, then our attention has little else to hold on to, other than to drift off or to attach itself to our bodily sensations:

> While reading this, switch your attention to the physical sensations of your skin, the feeling of your back against the chair, the sensation of the book against your fingers, your feet on the floor. It is possible to get so absorbed in these sensations, almost like sunbathing or lying in the bath, that nothing else seems to exist. You may find yourself closing your eyes. Otherwise they are likely to take on that glazed look which makes real seeing impossible, and where someone will invariably come waving their hand in front of your eyes saying 'Hey! Where have *you* gone?!' Sometimes just feeling looked at attentively brings someone, whose attention has drifted off, back into 'communicative mode', usually with a start, muttering something about 'Oh, I was just dreaming ...' And of course you *may* have been day-dreaming ...

However, basking in skin and bodily sensations is often not accompanied by day-dreaming, but devoid of mental activity, like a mental power-cut, with most brain activity switched off, almost like a temporary vegetative state. How much did you, for example, notice and take in what was going on around you, while focussing on the skin sensations on your chair, your back, shoulders, hands, feet? Did you see or hear anything? How much thinking was going on in your head? Probaby not much, or almost none. If you did this most of the day, how much would you hear, see, remember, or learn?

There is one big difference, though, between us doing this and the autistic child. While indulging in such bodily and skin sensations, you and I can think or even talk about our experience. In this way we assign meaning to our sensation experience, which turns pure sensual sensation, which is bathed or wallowed in, into feelings which can be thought about and communicated. The pre-verbal autistic child who has not learnt to speak and use symbols lacks this capacity, he is unable to process and think about his experiences in ways which we take for granted. Some seem to remain locked in some kind of sensual prison where their experience remains 'unmentalised'. Their mental equipment is developmentally like that of a very small baby, who too is largely dependent on making sense of the world through his bodily sensations, of feeling hungry or satisfied, bored or pleasurably stimulated, comfortable or insecurely held, warm and dry or wet, cold and dirty.

Because he is unable to think about things, which is a person's main way of holding on to their sense of self, the autistic child has to hold on to his physical and skin sensations at all times. Walking and being mobile may be a dodgy business to the autistic child who also wants to remain an 'inside baby', which the tiny baby, always held and carried, does not have to deal with. This certainly seemed to be the case with Kofi and Tim, who simply seemed to fall apart whenever they were not carried or held in someone's arms. Other autistic children appear to keep themselves in this sensation-dominated and mentally cut-off state much more deliberately, using their skin surface or other bodily sensations like a suit of armour to shield them from the awareness of the world around them.

Eryl made constant babbling noises so he could not hear anything anyone was saying to him. Later, when he began to speak, he did the same by repeating the same phrase over and over, thus drowning out all meaningful conversation. This stopped after about six months of intensive child psychotherapy. Eryl seemed to be so relieved to be offered the opportunity to learn to use his mind in different ways, and grasped this offer keenly.

These children find their main source of safety in the touch and sensations they experience against their skin, or like Eryl from the sensation of vibrations in his throat and sound in his ears. They seek comfort in sensations that are self-stimulated and self-controlled, rather than from a mothering person. Some autistic children appear to spend great chunks of each day practising these states of mental blankness by focussing on the bodily sensations, of their skin especially, and they may have been practising this for years, day-in, day-out, probably since their early baby days. They may not even know that there are other ways of being, other ways of looking, listening or feeling.

Because he does not link up sensation with meaning, the autistic child cuts off and avoids all awareness of feelings, yours as well as his own, and with this the possibility that anything could make any sense. Because he is so fixed on his skin sensations, the feelings that give meaning to sensory perceptions cannot be generated. It is as if his mind is on hold or standby, or has stalled. A vicious circle ensues, in which his sensation-dominated state does not equip him with means of relating to the world of aliveness and people; therefore his already delayed cognitive and emotional development dwindles even further as he defends himself against learning from other people, which further feeds his counterproductive autistic insistence on sensations to get rid of the awareness of any unknown and unpredictable aspects of life. Whether this is because of a fundamental insecurity in emotions (Dawson et al. 1994, Hobson 1993), a retreat to an emotionless world dominated by physical sensations, or because he has lost grip on the meaning of things and is unable to reassemble it by himself, no one knows.

If the autistic child's focus is on the sense of the impression the chair makes on his bottom, or the hard toy in his hand or against his lips, it can be very difficult to draw him out into some alternative experience which could be shared with another. The visual shapes and patterns used by some autistic children in the same sensual ways can more easily be made into a shareable experience, because we can see them too, and therefore deliberately provide and talk about them.

> Patrick liked the look and feel of completed puzzles, which allowed his key-worker repeatedly to show him the meaning of words such as 'finished', 'smooth', 'all done', as well as their opposites.
>
> Tyrone liked to look out of the window at the movements of a tree. This meant that it was possible to guess and put into words what he might be seeing, for instance the movement of branches or leaves, different rhythms of the wind, a squirrel or bird.

Other autistic children use sounds, or our talking to them, to bathe in, as in some kind of lullaby of musical sounds, never mind that those sounds are telling him to get up and join in, to look at the picture we are showing him, or that dinner is ready. This may be similar to Eryl's defensive use of sounds to ward off interference.

Keeping in mind the possibility that the autistic child may use his attention in sensation-dominated ways to focus on his skin or other bodily sensations allows us to have some idea where to meet him. If it is the sensations of his skin he gets absorbed by, we can introduce little communicative rhythms by patting on his arm or back, or stroking him in the rhythm of his movements or to that of a familiar song, giving him our undivided attention by naming for him what he sees or experiences, and by drawing him out into some more actively interactive games.

'He's So Good at Jigsaws and Puzzles': Patterns, Puzzles and Sensations

Autistic children are often very good at one particular cognitive skill, for example being surprisingly good at jigsaws and puzzles. Because of their overall developmental delay adults want to encourage and expand any such interests. Some will quickly reassemble any puzzle, whether upside down or back to front, while others insist on doing the same puzzle over and over, refusing to do any other. They seem as if driven from inside to do the puzzle with no sense of enjoyment or satisfaction while doing it, or any appreciation or even recognition of the finished picture.

> Tim's grim face and growling noises made it seem as if seeing this 'puzzle-thing' in such a mess irritated him greatly and he seemed to be reassembling it angrily and impatiently. He wouldn't dream of doing and undoing anything. He liked everything to be done up and stay just as it was.

It almost seemed as if Tim did a puzzle for the opposite reasons to us: we do a puzzle because we enjoy it; he seemed to do it precisely because he does *not* enjoy having anything to do with things like puzzles. The moment it is complete he wanders off, as if turning away quickly before seeing it messed up again. The fact that he had just created a picture of his favourite 'Thomas the Tank Engine' seemed to pass him by unnoticed! You and I and most other children do a puzzle or jigsaw because we are curious about the picture, enjoy being able to do it, or perhaps even that we can 'mend' something that has come undone. While we use a combination of the shapes of the puzzle-pieces and the bits that are missing from the picture, close observation of the autistic child's eye and body movements suggests that he often appears unaware of there being a picture at all. It seems as if it is not the emerging picture that guides him, but the outside shape of each piece regardless of colour or picture clues. In fact, he may have no awareness of the *meaning* of the emerging picture:

> His key-worker was delighted when Patrick became interested in puzzles. His concentration was total and he refused to stop even for drinks until it was completed. When his key-worker came to help him, he pushed her away vehemently, but was pleased when she later gave him another similar puzzle.

As he would not let her join him, she settled for trying to work out what it was that fascinated him so much, and we both sat to observe his body language carefully. If we watched his eyes and what exactly he was looking at before picking up a piece and how he went about trying to fit them together, then perhaps we would understand? We tried pointing out bits of colour to him, or bits of the picture that were missing or fitted together. But he angrily brushed us aside. He wanted to do it all by himself, and neither picture nor colour cues were what interested him. When we offered him the puzzle with the picture facing the table, he assembled it as quickly, if not more easily. Running his hand over the completed puzzle as if stroking it, his face would take on that far-away expression as if he were enjoying the sensation of its smoothness.

What distinguishes the autistic child's use of his eyes from ours, is that he does not use combinations of looking at shapes, colours and the emerging picture to put things together. Instead he 'feels it all over' with one glance in the way that blind people might sense its shape with the touch of their hands. Usually seeing is a *mental* activity, linked with thinking, which processes what is seen and makes sense of it. But for the autistic child it might be more like a visual sensation of a concrete kind, as if seeing were like 'touching with the eyes'. Patrick's stroking the completed puzzle perhaps shows how close seeing and sensual experience are to him. Seeing the puzzle undone seemed to be an almost physical experience to Tim that caused him actual pain which he quickly rid himself of – by doing it up. Patrick too liked its surface to be smooth and unbroken. More interested in the shapes and patterns, not what the puzzle was a picture of, both children seemed to experience the sight of the puzzle, undone or completed, in a way as if the sight left a physical impression in their mind as it would if held in their hand.

Other autistic children spend much of their day doing and undoing a puzzle, with the adults delighted to see so much of what seems like 'purposeful activity'. But the lack of a sense of enjoyment or satisfaction makes one wonder what the purpose of this puzzle activity might be. The adult is often faced with resistance when trying to help the child to expand this skill:

Susie carried her puzzle everywhere, doing and undoing it, at great speed. She refused to do anything else, no other puzzle or activity. Her teacher tried everything he could think of. Finally he decided that Susie had got truly stuck with that wretched old puzzle and that it prevented her from learning anything else. Desperate and at his wits end, he resorted to hiding it, thinking she'd soon forget and get used to doing other puzzles and activities. But no such luck! Instead Susie became anxious, withdrawn and cut-off with dreadful periods of desperate crying or angry attacks on herself and other people. Her teacher's attempts at comforting her with another similar puzzle also came to nothing. For a while it seemed as if it was now the teacher who had got himself stuck with an idea he was going to carry out whatever the cost. Eventually, despair took over and he felt a failure. His colleagues were also at a loss.

The staff team asked for an assessment from a child psychotherapist specialising in work with autistic children. Together they worked out that it was since her puzzle was taken away that Susie had become so distressed and anxious. The puzzle obviously served a different function from that of a cognitive activity. Susie *needed* the reassurance of the puzzle, of it being always the same, same shape, same pieces, same movements, to make her feel safe. When her teacher returned the original puzzle, Susie's behaviour and mood returned more or less to what it had been before. With the consultant's help the staff team came to see Susie's level of emotional–cognitive functioning more realistically and adapt their expectations: simply taking her puzzle away was not an option, but challenging her and expecting her to do other tasks was. (Spensley 1995)

It appears that it was not because she was particularly good at or fond of puzzles, but that to Susie doing and undoing her puzzle was perhaps a bit like another child sucking his thumb, holding on to his teddy or comfort blanket, fulfilling a similar function to Derek's jigging, Adrian's biting on a hard thing or Fred's clutching a small car. It was perhaps the comforting rhythm of doing and undoing her puzzle that was so all-important to Susie, because it occupied her mind so she did not have to think, feel or notice anything. But her teacher's sense that her puzzle activity prevented her from learning was of course correct: the autistic child engages in repetitive activities precisely to shut out any awareness. It so fills his mind that there is no room for worry or even for thinking: the comforting rhythm or sensations of the familiar always-the-same activity are all there is, and the activity itself becomes the whole of life, essential for survival and to be clung to at any cost.

Careful observation of autistic children suggests that they seem to see the world in terms of patterns and shapes that are abstract and special to each child. Often these are not geometric shapes we would recognise easily, but 'felt' shapes that are experienced as if they were a personal physical sensation: like Patrick's 'sensation' of the smoothness of the puzzle, the sensation of Derek's jigging, a child's 'sensation' of the colour red. The shapes and patterns which guide his experience are a similar concept to autistic objects, although more subtle and difficult to spot, because they are not concrete objects that are more directly visible. The autistic child uses all these to generate certain patterns of repeatable physical or visual sensations in his body, on his skin, or in his mind, to give him a sense of ongoingness and comfort (Tustin 1992, Spensley 1995).

> It took a lot of close observation until I discovered Leila's 'pattern': to have the bottom of containers covered with enough of the same sort of objects. What they were, their colour or position did not seem to matter, and it applied to any surface with some kind of rim, from trays, cups, containers, cardboard boxes to saucepans. Like Tim and Patrick, she too seemed to have an idea of a complete, unbroken surface with no 'holes'. She would carefully stack coloured reels into a tray with endless patience. But if there were not enough cotton-reels, little animals, wooden bricks, or whatever she was using at the time, then all hell would break loose. Once we knew what she was after, what her 'pattern' was, we could help her: she either needed more bricks, or a smaller-bottomed container! Easy, once you've done your homework of careful observation.

Such shared understanding and adaptions from an adult encourage the autistic child's interest in communication and in developing a sense of his own mind, of things making sense and having meaning. Our task is to be sensitive on two counts: first, to the child's need for the structure that is provided by these patterns of physical, visual or other bodily sensations. Then, we need to be alert and vigilant to a certain kind of deadness creeping in, of these shapes and patterns becoming the whole of his life. They have a tendency to take over, to swallow up the human aliveness of life, like damp or dry-rot creeping through the walls without anyone noticing it until it has permeated the building. Introducing little moments of fun together, using suspense and anticipation, singing and interactive games can drastically halt the progression of this kind of dry-rot or damp! Keep observing – but keep playing too!

Appendix

About the Nurseries and Schools

All the children in this book attended a nursery, playgroup or school in one of four inner-London boroughs, usually full time. Among these were several mainstream nurseries, an integrated playgroup and an autistic unit for twelve children, attached to a school for children with moderate learning difficulties, where I worked for over two years. Teachers here used a number of structured and behavioural methods in the classroom, but also actively supported child psychotherapy for some of the children where this was found to be appropriate and helpful by parents and school.

About half of the children described in this book attended a special needs nursery for eight children with communication difficulties, including autism and speech/language disorders, where I worked as a play-specialist for over six years with the children and the five nursery workers. We found that it was crucial for each child to have a key-worker (and a back-up), an individual play programme tailored specifically to each child's developmental level (taking into account what parents were most concerned about), specific guidance to each key-worker on how to implement these programmes and deal with difficult behaviours, and a clear but varied daily structure to the nursery day. Home visits were also crucial to allow the key-worker to have an idea of what kind of expectation of the world each child was bringing in his mind (for example whether very strict and organised, or from a home with very little furniture, no toys, no garden, no stimulation, or from a large, lively family in a comfortable house).

About the Children

In the following descriptions, all confidential details have been omitted or changed in order to ensure the anonymity of families, who come from many different cultural backgrounds.

Adrian (three years) lives with his parents and sixteen-year old brother. He was born in this country shortly after his father had a nearly fatal accident which left him unable to pursue his profession as an artist. He took greater interest in Adrian, carrying him around, than his mother who was often preoccupied with her part-time work.

Anushka (nine to ten months) was the first baby to parents who had been waiting for her for many years. Her father worked as a management consultant, while her mum stayed at home devoting all her time to being and playing with Anushka.

Billy (seven years) spent much of his infancy and childhood in front of the TV and video, which his politically very active mother says he liked. His parents are busy professionals and their two children are now at residential schools in Cornwall.

Cheng (four years) has an older sister who is doing well at school. They live with their parents who both work full time. Cheng's mother says that when he was a baby, Cheng was so small that she used to hide him in another room, being too ashamed to let visitors see him. Later she felt both ashamed and unable to manage to take him out, as he would kick his shoes off every few steps on the street.

Clive (eight years) has an older sister who was devoted to him until she was about fourteen (and became very insecure), at a time when Clive became more forceful and difficult. Their father, a reserved, quiet man who takes Clive on outings at weekends, works for the local council, their mother is assertive but socially shy and works part time in a shop.

Derek (four years) used to cling to people as if in fright when younger, but loved being invited into little interactive games. His softly spoken mother was on anti-depressants after Derek's as well as his younger brother's birth, feeling unsupported by her husband, who later tried to make Derek into a 'real boy' by shouting and threatening him with his belt. Mother has since completed a training course, is full of confidence, working full time and considering sending Derek to residential school.

Eryl (six years) seemed to have found his father's moving out, after many arguments and fights, much more difficult than his slightly older sister, and became difficult, uncooperative and contrary. His teachers at an autistic unit helped him greatly by being both understanding and strict about boundaries. He later learnt to speak and read, but used the 'noise' of his own speaking for a long time as a 'sound wall' to ward off communication.

After about six months of psychotherapy, he became much happier in himself, keen to cooperate and began to talk about his experiences.

Fatima (five years) was the younger of two girls, living in her mother's student digs with both parents, who always worked full time, her father as an academic, her mother, who had been orphaned at an early age, as a health professional. Although both parents seemed to have little understanding for their children, they eventually sought long-term psychotherapeutic help for the family.

Fred (four years) was one of those highly anxious, insecure children who when little was happy to be left alone in a room for long periods. He was very attached to his dad who did all the caring and worrying about him and his brother. His mother had little relationship with either boy, and she never came to nursery to see him there or meet his workers. When pregnant again, she was anxious for it to be a girl.

Gary (three years) lived alone with his elderly mother, who could not understand why school said that it was not possible for them to get food every day from Burger King for Gary's dinner, which she said was all he ate.

Harvey (four years) and his seven-year-old brother live with their rather strict parents who have high expectations of their children. Their mother works part time as a classroom assistant in a primary school, their dad is a caretaker. The family have a good social network of extended family and friends.

Jazzy (four years) had a new baby sister when I knew him and was the wildest whirlwind I had ever met, always on the run as if frantically running away from anything that could be getting at him. He lived with several large dogs, his young mum and somewhat intimidating father in a mysterious house full of shutters and security locks. Mum looked kind, helpless and occasionally bruised. When I met her about two years later, she had had another baby, and reported that Jazzy was doing well, was talking and had become an ordinary boy.

Jenny (three months) was the first baby of a single mother with emotional and learning difficulties. At the age of one year Jenny was adopted because of emotional and physical neglect, and is now thriving.

Kofi (three years) was the much-loved result of a short-lived relationship. Until he was almost four they lived at the house of his grandmother, who adored him, with several aunties and uncles who carried him all the time, whether he cried or not, despite his mother's protests to give him some space and time just to be.

Leila (four years) had been 'funny' already as a baby, her mother reports, suddenly making herself go stiff or rocking her baby-bouncer so violently that Mum was worried it may tip over. Her older brother would comment that 'She's staring at me!' when Leila was less than one year old, and the family feared that she may be possessed by evil spirits. Leila's father's whereabouts were unknown, which may have had political reasons. Leila always struck me as a very imaginative child full of (sometimes fixed) ideas and phantasies, but at the same time extremely wilful, determined and powerful. Her mother had a feelingful relationship with her son but felt out of her depth with Leila's unforgivingness.

Max (five years) was an adored only son of parents who spoke little English, and found it very hard to understand both their son and the ways of this country. He seemed to terrorise them somewhat at home with his endless climbing and screaming, which they did not know how to stop, and later, at a highly acclaimed special school, he caused grave concerns by constantly running away.

Mohamed (six years) was the oldest of five children with very down-to-earth commonsensical parents. His dad worked full time, his mother looked after the children and seemed to have no problem being clear about boundaries while at the same time allowing for Mohamed's special difficulties where necessary.

Mustafa (two years) was a little boy I only met a few times when visiting another nursery. His disability did not affect his communication and he is not on the autistic continuum.

Nelson (five years) was a headstrong young character but riddled with terrible anxieties. While frequently obstinate and insistent on not cooperating with his teachers whatever the consequences, he seemed terrified of making sounds. His dad discovered a way to get Nelson to speak, and for about two years Nelson would speak 'into his hand', initially only if the adult said the words into his hand and then held it to Nelson's mouth. There were two older siblings, but Nelson was clearly the baby and at the same time entirely 'in charge'.

Patrick (five years) was born a year after his eight-month-old sister had died from cot death. He now has two younger brothers, one of whom may also be autistic. His father is very strict, his mother is loving but unsure of how to bring children up without an extended family. She is still hoping for a girl to be born.

Ryan (four years) was the first child born in this country to a single mother who left two older sons in Africa with family in order to learn about cake-decorating in this country. He spent his first years with numerous neighbours and childminders while Mum worked long hours. At the age of five he had been excluded from five nurseries for unmanageable behaviour, and finally went to live in a foster-family, attending a special school. At the age of seven, he has caught up with his language development, is beginning to play symbolically and relates well to his peers, teachers and foster-relatives.

Simon (seven years) has a younger sister and lives with his parents who are committed but reserved, keeping their personal details to themselves. I believe his father works full time, while his mother is at home and his sister is a bright little button.

Tashan (four years) lived with his mum, who is unemployed, and later his younger sister. He sees his father occasionally. He was always willing to cooperate, and finally went on to a special school where he is doing well.

Terry (five years) and his older sister live with their mum and dad, who works as a car mechanic. His mum says he was already hyperactive as a baby, and that she had to bottle and spoon feed him all the time to keep him quiet. If thwarted Terrry would fly into violent frenzies of attacking other people with hands, teeth and 'claws'.

Tim (three years) lived with his parents who both worked full time and were, like his older brother, gifted musicians. During the day he was looked after by various nannies. At home nothing was asked of him, and he spent much time 'watching' videos. Around the age of five, I was told that he had started to bite his hand when asked to do something. He went on to go to a highly regarded autistic school, where teachers struggle to get him to do anything.

Tyrone (five years) lives with his older sister and his mum who does not work. His sister also had difficulties with her speech/language development, but is now doing well at school. His father is around somehow, but I never found out whether he lives with them or not.

Yusuf (four years) lived with his three brothers and his mother, who was always terrified that her violent husband may come back and attack her again. In her utter helplessness she often left Yusuf alone in the house in order to attend to school issues concerning her other children, one of whom has similar difficulties to Yusuf.

Bibliography

Aarons, M. et al. (1991) *The Handbook of Autism: A Guide for Parents and Professionals*. London: Routledge.
—— (1992) *The Autistic Continuum*. Windsor: NFER-Nelson.
Alvarez, A. (1992) *Live Company*. London: Routledge.
Alvarez, A. and Reid, S. (1999) *Autism and Personality*. London: Routledge.
Attwood, T. *Why Does Chris Do That?* London: NAS.
Baron-Cohen, S. et al. (1993) *Autism: The Facts*. Oxford: Oxford University Press.
—— (1993) *Understanding Other Minds: Perspectives from Autism*. Oxford: Oxford University Press.
Barron, J. and S. (1993) *There's a Boy in Here*. London: Chapmans.
Bick, E. (1968) Experience of the Skin in Early Object Relations. In: *International Journal of Psychology*, 49.
—— (1986) Further Considerations on the Function of the Skin in Early Object Relations. In: *British Journal of Psychotherapy*, 2.
Bion, W. (1962) *Learning From Experience*. London: Heinemann.
Bion, W. (1967) A Theory of Thinking. In: *Second Thoughts*. London: Heinemann.
Brazelton, B. et al. (1974) The Origins of Reciprocity. In: E. Lewis et al. *The Effect of the Infant on His Caregivers*. London: Wiley.
Bruner, J. et al. (1976) Peekaboo and the Learning of Rule Structures. In: *Play*. Harmondsworth: Penguin.
Bullowa, M. (1979) *Before Speech: The Beginnings of Human Communication*. London: Cambridge University Press.
Carpenter, G. (1974) Mother's Face and the Newborn. In: *New Scientist*, March.
Dawson, G. et al. (1994) *Human Behaviour and the Developing Brain*. New York: Guilford Press.
Dornes, M. (1993) *Der kompetente Säugling*. Frankfurt: Fischer.

Dzikowski, S. (1993) *Ursachen des Autismus*. Weinheim: Deutscher Studienverlag.

Eggers, C. et al. (1994) *Kinder- und Jugendpsychiatrie*. Berlin: Springer Verlag.

Eliacheff, C. (1993) *A corps et a cris. Etre psychanalyste avec les tout-petits*. Ed. Odile Jacob.

Freeman, N. et al. (1980) Hide and Seek Is Child's Play. In: *New Scientist*, 88.

Frith, U. (1989) *Autism: Explaining the Enigma*. Oxford: Blackwell.

Gesell, A. (1943) *The Mental Growth of the Preschool Child*. New York: Macmillan.

Grandin, T. et al. (1986) *Emergence Labelled Autistic*. Tunbridge Wells: Costello.

Griffiths, P. (1996) Paediatric Neuropsychology. In: *The Psychologist*, November.

Hobson, P.R. (1993) *Autism and the Development of Mind*. Hove: Lawrence Erlbaum.

Hocking, B. (1990) *Little Boy Lost*. London: Bloomsbury.

Klauber, T. (1993) personal communication.

Lempp, R. (1992) *Vom Verlust der Fähigkeit sich selbst zu betrachten*. Bern: Huber.

—— (1996) *Die autistische Gesellschaft*. München: Kösel.

Meltzer, D. et al. (1975) *Explorations in Autism*. Strath Tay: Clunie Press.

Mesibov, B. (1993) Inductive Course to TEACCH ('Treatment and Education of Autistic and Communication Handicapped Children'). University of North Carolina.

Murray, L. (1992) The Impact of Post-Natal Depression on Infant Development. *Journal of Child Psychology and Psychiatry*, 33 (3).

Murray, L. and Trevarthen, C. (1985) Emotional Regulation of Interactions Between 2-Month-Olds and Their Mothers. In: T. Field and N. Fox. *Social Perception in Infants*. Norwood, N.J.: Ablex.

Newson, E. (1999) 'Coherence out of the Fragments of Autism', paper given at conference in Oxford.

Ogden, T. (1992) *The Primitive Edge of Experience*. London: Karnac.

Olson, D. (1980) *The Social Foundations of Language and Thought*. New York: Norton.

Prevezer, W. (1990) Strategies for Tuning into Autism. In: *Therapy Weekly*, October.

—— (1991) Musical Interaction. In: *Speech and Language Disorder Newsletter*, 37.

Reddy, V. (1992) Playing with Others' Expectations: Teasing and Mucking about in the First Year. In: A. Whiten *Natural Theories of Mind*. Oxford: Blackwell.

Ricks, D. and Wing, L. (1975) Language, Communication, and the Use of Symbols in Normal and Autistic Children. In: *Journal of Autism and Childhood Schizophrenia*, 5, 3.

Schaffer, H.R. (1977) *Studies in Mother–Infant Interaction*. London: Academic Press.

Schopler, E. et al. (1993) *Preschool Issues in Autism*. New York: Plenum.

—— (1994) *Behavioural Issues in Autism*. New York: Plenum.

Schopler, E. (1995) *Parent Survival Manual*. New York: Plenum.

Spensley, S. (1985) Cognitive Deficit, Mindlessness and Psychotic Depression. *Journal of Child Psychotherapy*, 1 (3).

—— (1995) *Frances Tustin*. London: Routledge.

Stern, D. (1977) *The First Relationship: Infant and Mother*. Cambridge MA: Harvard University Press.

—— (1985) *The Interpersonal World of the Infant*. New York: Basic Books.

—— (1991) *Diary of a Baby*. New York: Basic Books.

Tager-Flusberg, H. (1981) On the Nature of Linguistic Functioning in Early Autism. *Journal of Autism and Developmental Disorders*, 11.

Trevarthen, C. (1977) Descriptive Analyses of Infant Communicative Behaviour. In: H.R. Schaffer *Studies in Mother–Infant Interaction*. London: Academic Press.

—— (1979) Communication and Cooperation in Early Infancy. In: M. Bullowa *Before Speech: The Beginnings of Human Communication*. London: Cambridge University Press.

—— (1980) The Foundations of Intersubjectivity. In: D. Olson *The Social Foundations of Language and Thought*. New York: Norton.

—— (1985) Facial Expressions of Emotion in Mother–Infant Interaction. *Human Neurobiology*, 4.

Trevarthen, C. et. al. (1996) *Children with Autism*. London: Jessica Kingsley.

Tustin, F. (1981, 1992) *Autistic States in Children*. London: Tavistock/Routledge.

—— (1986) *Autistic Barriers in Neurotic Patients*. London: Karnac.

—— (1990) *The Protective Shell in Children and Adults*. London: Karnac.

Whiten, A. (1992) *Natural Theories of Mind*. Oxford: Blackwell.

Williams, D. (1992) *Nobody Nowhere*. London: Doubleday.

—— (1994) *Somebody Somewhere*. London: Doubleday.

—— (1996) *Autism: An Inside-Out Approach*. London: Jessica Kingsley.

—— (1996) *Like Colour to the Blind*. New York: Times Books.

Wing, L. (1992) *Autistic Spectrum Disorders: An Aid to Diagnosis*. London: NAS.

—— (1996) *The Autistic Spectrum: Guide for Parents and Professionals*. London: Constable.

Index

Compiled by Sue Carlton